My Heart is Ready

My Heart is Ready

Feasts and Fasts

on Fifth Avenue

John Andrew

COWLEY PUBLICATIONS
Cambridge ✦ Boston
Massachusetts

Published in the United States of America by Cowley Publications, a division of the Society of St. John the Evangelist. No portion of this book may be reproduced, stored in or introduced into a retrieval system, or transmitted, in any form or by any means—including photo-copying—without the prior written permission of Cowley Publications, except in the case of brief quotations embodied in critical articles and reviews.

Library of Congress Cataloging in Publication Data:
Andrew, John, Rev., Dr.
My heart is ready: feasts and fasts on Fifth Avenue / John Andrew
p.   cm.
ISBN 1-56101-108-8 (alk. paper).
ISBN 1-56101-107-X (pbk.: alk. paper)
1. Church year sermons.   2. Sermons, American.   3. Episcopal Church—Sermons.   4. Anglican Communion—United States—Sermons. I. Title.
BX5937.A53M8   1995
252'.6—dc20   94-41666
                                                      CIP

The photograph of the altar frontal from Saint Thomas Fifth Avenue was taken by Richard F. Mullen, who graciously gave permission for its use on this book. Cover design and copyediting by Vicki Black.

Scripture quotations are taken from the King James Version, the Revised Standard Version, and the New English Bible.

This book is printed on recycled, acid-free paper and was produced in the United States of America.

Cowley Publications
28 Temple Place
Boston, Massachusetts 02111

This book is dedicated to Bishop Michael Marshall,
one of our century's great preachers,
who upholds Catholic truth with evangelical fervor,
and through his episcopate in the Anglican Church
has guarded and enriched the faith
with learning, devotion, and a lively spirit.

Table of Contents

LENT

MAUNDY THURSDAY

GOOD FRIDAY

EASTER EVE

EASTERTIDE

PENTECOST

CHRIST THE KING

Acknowledgments

My patient and cheerful secretary, Georgiana Aybar, is much enjoyed by all my parishioners and colleagues for her ready friendliness and disposition to help. She is one of the few people who refuse to make heavy weather of my handwriting: week by week she tackles the Sunday sermon manuscript with dispatch. Upon her has fallen the burden of typing and collating the sermons for this book. I want very much to thank her for doing this, *as well as* seeing that the ongoing tasks of the parish office are promptly and efficiently undertaken.

To be encouraged to put together a third collection of sermons for publication leaves me indebted to my friends, and especially another Michael in my life after Archbishop Michael Ramsey: Michael Marshall, Bishop in the Church of God, a glorious preacher who is much loved and admired by my wonderful family on Fifth Avenue.

Foreword

For twenty-two years now, over a third of my life, it has been my privilege to minister to a remarkable parish family on Fifth Avenue, New York, by word and sacrament. To have such a ravishingly beautiful church so strategically placed in this noisy and combative city is exciting, certainly, and more. Saint Thomas' staggering and welcoming dignity, full of architectural triumphs—the height of its roof and its carved limestone reredos, or altar screen; the deep Chartres blue of its stained and painted glass windows; the thunder of music from the fine organ cases; the great bronze statue of Our Lady of Fifth Avenue, listening for the prayers of the faithful to her Son as she sits with her head turned slightly to one side, evoke awe *and* acceptance, both. Why this should be so is a mystery. But people will tell you about the atmosphere of the place, and when in the liturgies crowds come in and find they can sing to their hearts' content and pray and listen joyfully, catching the exhilaration of the worship we try to offer, they leave the better and richer for it.

Preaching is treated with respect here by those of us who do it and those who share in it. Frankly, I have to *slave* at sermons. You would think that after thirty-eight years in the priesthood certain things would come more easily, like preaching. I do not find this so. I am haunted by the fear of sounding stale. Notice that I did not say *re-*

petitive. A preacher must be repetitive, in order to bang nails firmly home. I make no apology for that. The art is to re-present the thrill of the gospel imaginatively, cogently, and accurately. It takes all I have to try to maintain this ideal.

People help: their experiences, their fears, their frustrations, their fulfillments, and their triumphs of grace in their lives are a wellspring of inspiration. "All my fresh springs shall be in thee" is a phrase from the psalms that I know to be true in my life as a priest and friend and teacher and preacher. Seeing Christ living in my beloved family members here at Saint Thomas is a great corrective for dullness and self-concern. Books help, too. I always have several going at once, all different: theology, biography, poetry, art, mystery novels, history.

But you have to be on the look-out for parables too, and they sprout everywhere: in shop-window displays; on the sides of buses; in street exchanges between myriad kinds of humanity; in situations where there is humor to be found; on the television; around the supper table; in museum exhibitions or in the theater. I think you get into the habit of picking up on things; certainly my friends will observe that I might pocket such and such an incident or remark for a sermon. "Take care!" they warn. "He'll use it in the pulpit!" Often, true.

You can gather that though I regard sermon preparation as a burden, it is never a *chore*. It is, I suppose, a costly delight; I love it but it takes its toll. And it is an honor. One good word is not as good as another, and every word has to be written and balanced and assimilated. There is a curious accolade of honor bestowed on the person who can "preach without notes," as if somehow the message is worth more for its invisible source of delivery.

In fact, the only preacher in this category I know who is worth listening to with unalloyed pleasure and unflagging concentration is John Maury Allin, our extraordinary former Presiding Bishop and Primate. He is a tower of integrity and humility both, who learned this rare craft in prison, as he told me: notes before the preacher in prison chapel distract the prisoners. I can see why, but I can't do it myself.

Not least am I helped by my colleagues, often much younger than myself. The presence among us at Saint Thomas of a lively and very amusing young priest with real homiletic *punch* has earned my gratitude increasingly in the two years he has served here. I look forward to hearing him every time he preaches.

I also need to pay tribute to the Sunday congregations who have challenged us preachers with their keen attention and critical support, their intelligence and their encouragement. We have a great deal for which to thank God.

ADVENT

Advent is the beginning of the church's year. The Scripture lessons and prayers for this season of preparation for the feast of Christmas are often reflective of divine judgment and our penitence, as well as the hope of Christ's coming.

The last of these three sermons for Advent was delivered at the Festival of Lessons and Carols on the last Sunday before Christmas.

The
Road Makers

I think you would agree with me that every age can have its share of eccentricity in appearance. At the corner of 57th Street and Fifth Avenue I watched a determined young woman in a long mink coat stride into the traffic. She had a baseball cap on her head and was wearing white sneakers and black athletic tights. You might say she was setting a style.

The surgeon to King Louis XIV, M. de l'Orme, says Nancy Mitford in her book *The Sun King*, mystified that extraordinary court in Versailles, for he was covered "with a morocco robe and mask and wore six pairs of stockings and several fur hats. He always kept a bit of garlic in his mouth, incense in his ears, and a stalk of rue sticking out of each nostril."

You heard about John the Baptist in the gospel for today, Luke 3:1-6. John was wild. The people thought so. He refused to live in a house in a town. He lived in a hole somewhere in the scrub and rock outside the town. He refused to dress. He wrapped a length of camel-hair cloth around him, Matthew tells us, with a leather belt to keep it up. He ate organic food only: wild honey and locusts.

As a solitary mystic, John had been far more accustomed to talking to God than arguing about the points of
the Mosaic Law with the scribes. He had waited upon the
Lord to renew his strength—and God had renewed it. He
was not merely a kindred spirit of Isaiah the prophet; he
was Isaiah's mouthpiece to his generation, the fulfillment
in himself of Isaiah's prophecy of the voice crying in the
wilderness, "Prepare ye the way of the Lord! Make
straight in the desert a highway for our God!" He had
Isaiah under his skin, if you like. He knew perhaps just
this: that he must say something to his contemporaries by
way of a warning because something was going to happen:
a cataclysm.

What John does as a preacher must have since given
every professor in the art of preaching a fit, beginning
with Saint Augustine. When you get up to preach you
don't first hit your hearers over the ears with anything
that comes to hand; you "capture their goodwill," as
Augustine instructs us. You say something that will turn
them on, in other words, not turn them off. But John, this
shaggy figure, would have failed the homiletics courses at
the General Theological Seminary or any other place because he launches into a tirade of abuse. He doesn't begin,
"My friends." He calls them "You bunch of snakes!"

He has watched the adders sunning themselves on the
rocks in the hot sun of the desert, near their nests. He has
watched them produce their young. He has seen them,
lazy in the sunshine, and he tells the people who gather
around him that they are like those snakes, and where are
they going to slither off to when the fire comes? And who
does he say this to? He says it to the respected, learned,
linen-clad Pharisees—the religious establishment. Not
that John could care. He punctures their complacency. He

winds them. He insults their assumptions. He tells them that the sky will fall in before they realize it, and it will be all their fault.

John is absolutely fearless and he is absolutely unsparing. The nation of Israel managed to convey to the countries surrounding them the impression that they regarded themselves as special, favored, unique in the affections of God, singled out for divine protection, superior to their pagan neighbors, and altogether impossible to get along with. They were determined; they had a mission in life. They had a story to tell, a history to recount, which gave them an horizon to make for, a path and a purpose to pursue. They had a sense of destiny, for they were what they were because of a solemn agreement with their God. Nothing could shake their conviction that they were special, they were true, and they were right.

And they had the fixed notion that their progress to their divine destiny and everlasting blessedness was on automatic pilot. God had made his home with *them*. That same Lord would one day suddenly come to his Temple, the house they had built for him, and meanwhile they would wait. When he would come there would be judgment and the rest of humanity would pay for its failure to see things exactly in the way they saw things; they, and only they, would escape the divine wrath.

Adders sunning on a rock. Lazy snakes. And John pitches in. What you need, he says, and you need it now, is a little less self-congratulation and a great deal more self-examination. The favorite indoor game of plugging loopholes in the Law will not save you Pharisees or make the nation water-tight from the flood of the divine wrath. What you need is to say you're sorry, to turn back and to seek the living Lord with fruits of repentance. Wake up!

Shape up! Repent and come through the waters of baptism to be cleansed and refreshed for the task.

The task. To prepare the way of the Lord; make straight in the desert a highway for our God. The trouble was, Israel thought it had arrived; there was no serious roadmaking left to do. Israel wasn't prepared to be told that the axe was laid at the root of the trees not producing good fruit, and a fire was burning for the chaff separated by the winnowing fork from the wheat that God was harvesting.

Hundreds of years before, Isaiah had written of

> The voice of one crying in the wilderness,
>> Prepare ye the way of the Lord,
> Make straight in the desert
>> a highway for our God.

It is the mantle placed upon the shoulders of every generation since. No believer can evade the role.

We have difficulty with this concept. In the snobbish way we do things and think of things, there are groups of people we classify as being in a stratum beneath our notice. One such group is those who make and mend the roads. Because we are racist at heart we think of bulky red-faced Irishmen whom the English unpardonably call "navvies," or of the employment of trusted prisoners under the care and surveillance of wardens armed with a rifle in the South. Road makers don't stand high in any civilization. Around the Pearl Harbor anniversary this year I found myself thinking of the thousands of our allied military men captured by the Japanese later in the war and put to slavery under brutal conditions to build the Burma Road. As they dropped to their starved, exhausted, and diseased deaths, their bones became part of that infamous track through jungle and rock. Nothing, to my mind, brings memories harder to forgive or to forget than the use of young humanity by force and cruelty to create something they have no aptitude for.

I stood in the Holy Land on the top of the ancient fort at Masada one burning day in August last year where an ancient community of recklessly valiant and defiant Jews had held out against the Roman occupation forces until what could be the world's largest ramp or sloping road had been built against the cliffs to reach the fort, built with callous speed using slave labor. How many died making it? Thousands.

Road makers aren't heroes. They are functionaries. Expendable. Curiously and to our great discomfort, God sees us as such. It is what we are supposed to be about. You might wonder what valleys are to be filled and what mountains are to be felled. The bleak fact is that the existing landscape has to be changed for the Lord. It needs to be changed, so that the things that identify it are no longer in place. What about the valleys of ignorance, of illiteracy, of poverty which exist in this city alone? The hungers that never seem to be fed, not only for food but also for justice; the marginalized, the discriminated against; those who are sick and who die alone? What about the mountains of uncaring from greedy landlords in New York? Or the drug-traffickers' profits from the young?

To live here oblivious of them is to live in the past—the far past—the days of John the Baptist. Christ wants our compassion and our concern for the issues that cause hurt and damage to the least of these his little ones. What we do from here can only scratch the surface, we might say. But our efforts may dislodge a stone in the way of the

Lord's path, or a pothole may be filled if we manage, for instance, to get a relationship right or bring a loved one to terms with his addiction, or put an apology in the place where we have caused hurt needlessly, or return something we owe, or restore something we have stolen, like a reputation we have slandered.

It is the readiness to be used which God wants from us, for his kingdom is built upon penitence and humility and generosity of heart and forgiveness and willingness to start again.

Road makers for the Lord! There is much to be done. For Christ's sake, let us get on with it!

The
Dawning

Waiting can be a devastating experience. I have just put down Terry Waite's book, *Taken on Trust*, written after four long years of solitary confinement in some stinking hole in Beirut after being taken as a hostage by the Hezbollah.

Can you imagine? Chained by the ankle for years, without daylight, forbidden to talk aloud except to his Lebanese guards, and that only to make requests or answer an angry question. No books for two years. No pen, no paper; no radio, no television until near the end of his incarceration. Just himself, a blanket, a blindfold to be put on every time the door was unlocked, a thin mattress. And a chain. With mosquitoes and cockroaches for company. No calendar to mark the seasons, no watch to tell the time, until it was restored to him within the last few months before his release. No way of knowing what the weather was like or when, if ever, release and freedom would come to him.

It was a *suspended animation* which he withstood as best he could with interior and mental exercises rehearsed and silently practiced, and his autobiography begun and written in his head and in his heart. All he could do was to

wait; sitting, in chains, with a slow death from lung disease and blindness as a distinct possibility along that road
of waiting. *It is a nightmare of a story of prison existence.*

But prison existence isn't always limited to physical incarceration. Have you not felt the steel bands of fear
around you when you hear of senseless violence close to
home, of the Long Island Railroad massacre of commut-
ers, whose lives were extinguished by a madman? Isn't
this country in some sort of captivity to gun laws that allow fearsome killing weapons into the hands of *anybody,*
honest or criminal, who wishes to possess them? What is
wrong with our thinking on this point? Shootings in-
crease around us. Faithful worshipers here are now terrified of the journey into the city, where they feel they may
be mown down. They are manacled by fear of violence.
Look at parents of school children in St. Louis and Cali-
fornia, where beautiful little girls have been attacked and
murdered. Those parents are in a dungeon, helpless with
apprehension. They feel alone and without recourse. Fear
imprisons. Waiting in fear makes hours endless. *It is a
nightmare of a story of prison existence.*

You have only to read the numbing account of San
Francisco, now sitting captive in the darkness of apprehension as the AIDS epidemic seems mysteriously to
gather pace after years of a dramatic holding-pattern. We
are told that there is, experts summarize, a *psychology of
despair* that leads people to say, what the hell? and recklessly jettison precaution. "All of us are going to die one
day," they say, and despair possibly drives them into what
is, when you think of it, suicide. *It is a nightmare of a story
of prison existence.*

On the face of things, the countries at war within themselves are imprisoned in struggles without end or reason;

ancient hatreds and historic injuries shackle all attempts
to make peace in what was Bosnia and Serbia or Somalia
or the Sudan or Northern Ireland. *It is a nightmare of a
story of prison existence.*

Imprisonment, prison existence, has many forms and
many faces. This mysterious season of Advent is as good a
time as any in the year to contemplate it in the setting of
the approach of Christ our King, our Savior and our
Judge, who brings liberation from fear and from the inertia of despair. You may remember a hymn you have sung
here:

> He comes the prisoners to release
> in Satan's bondage held;
> The gates of brass before him burst,
> the iron fetters yield.

His approach is as inexorable as the threats to our
world peace, our personal safety, the health of our nation,
and the well-being of our children. He comes because his
love is unstoppable, as unstoppable as the first light of
dawn follows the dark of the night. He *is* the personifica-
tion of that superb verse in the Psalms:

> Mercy and truth are met together,
> righteousness and peace
>   have kissed each other. (Psalm 85:10)

Christ claims to be the Truth—"I am the way, the truth,
and the life" (John 14:6). His righteousness, based upon
his truth, is at the very heart of all justice and integrity,
and his justice *is* his mercy. He brings his peace "to you
which were afar off, and to them that were nigh," and
when he reconciles us to God through himself, "he *is* our
peace" (Ephesians 2:14,17).

Christ *is* our liberation, the opener of our dungeon doors, the breaker of the gates of brass that shut us in from him and from each other. Christians have held tenaciously to this through persecution, fire, and sword. They have laid their lives on the line with this conviction. They have defied threats and blackmail with that unshakable certainty: blessed assurance, you can call it. God's good *will* triumph; Christ *has* won; the waiting and the anxieties notwithstanding.

Some of you have heard me tell a story of my former parish, Preston, in Lancashire. At the time in our history when Roman Catholics were being hunted down like rats and exterminated after torture, a young priest was caught and dragged to London for execution. The news of his arrest got to his mother's town, Preston, and the citizens stormed the parish church to get to the belfry, where they started to toll the bell for his death. His mother, Mrs. Greenhalgh, clawed her way up the spiral stairs through the mob and reached the belfry, where she shouted: "Not a toll! Not a toll! Ring a peal, for I have borne a martyr unto God." She knew how to rejoice.

Which we do today, *Gaudete,* the first glimmers of the dawn of Christ's appearing:

> For lo, already on the hills
>   the flags of dawn appear;
> Gird up your loins, ye Prophet souls!
>   Proclaim the day is near!

> The day in whose clear shining light
>   all wrong shall stand revealed;
> When justice shall be throned in might,
>   And ev'ry hurt be healed.

This is no polyanna preaching—I would not dare to insult you this way. This isn't so much a story with a happy ending as it is a recognition of Christ's own victory after the hard-won fight of the cross. This is God in action, God moving toward us as he lives in us, undeterred by injustice and wickedness and the schemers of untruth, taking us along with him, in his purposes of love.

It is necessary for balance in the Christian faith to be able to say with the psalmist:

> The Lord hath done great things for us;
> whereof we are glad. (Psalm 126:3)

And rejoicing, we look forward, as members of the Advent church, loyal and alive to God. This of all days is "the day which the Lord hath made." We proclaim it Rejoicing Sunday, *Gaudete*, to a world suspicious of and cynical at the constant and continuing hash we make of what we affirm. And, despite our sins, failures, and negligences, with those who claim Christ's company we await the day

> When knowledge, hand in hand with peace
> Shall walk the earth abroad;
> The Day of perfect righteousness,
> The Promised Day of God.

God and Garbage Disposal

Slowly but surely we are becoming conservation-minded. We are required to sort out the cans from the paper, the bottles from the stale food. We are learning it the hard way. The hardest way conceivable, when a conscientious, loving, caring shepherd of a head teacher walks into the crossfire of a drug gun battle while he is looking for a child who has run away. It is waste of the most appalling kind. A life. A good life. An example. A light for people to see by. A hope for people to hang on to. Some are contemptuous of human disability. They don't even bother to sort the garbage of what was God's image and likeness as women are raped and men are mown down. Our streets are littered with unsorted garbage of humanity: those who are homeless clog the sidewalks, and nobody knows what to do with the mess.

No new phenomenon, this. Sadly, people have always done this to each other, ignorant of God's will and wish that his creation sing in harmony, ignorant that life-waste is a moral problem.

The astonishing thing is this: God has intervened by making himself a disposable item. God places himself right among the life-waste. His son is born homeless. In a

cave, at the mercy not merely of the elements but of occu-
pying forces who see him and his parents as a digit on a
chart in a census for tax purposes. Vulnerable to poverty,
repression, exclusion, uncaring whims and anonymous
extinction. This is how Saint John describes it:

> God so loved the world that he gave his only begotten
> Son, to the end that all who believe in him should not
> perish, but have everlasting life. (John 3:16)

Here, and here to stay. God with us. Here to stay among
the human predicament of capacity for suffering from
marginalization, rejection, relegation to the garbage heap
of humanity; utterly disposable, anonymous, and a nuisance to those who don't want to be bothered by people
whose poverty gets in their way. So you see him in the
eyes of babies despairing of food in the midst of famine.
You see him in the bent head of a mother mourning over
the grave of her son killed in battle, you see him in the
tears of the black child crying for his head teacher, Patrick Daly, in the Red Hook housing project. And you also
see him in the hands of the famine relief worker photographed caressing a small child and giving her a hug, in
the concerned faces of those who are determined that
peace shall once again come to war-torn countries, in the
voice of New York's mayor who tells the grieving in the
projects that the school children are Patrick Daly's living
memorials, and in the posters drawn by the young people
there proclaiming that they love him still.

Christmas time reminds us that God has views on garbage disposal; that he is the heart and soul of conserva-
tion of life in the world. He ensures that by intervening
personally: by placing himself in his son among it all, to

live among it, and finally to save it—by being disposed of. He has plans for us. And waste is not part of them.

Never forget this. Who is it but Christ who could tell his friends after feeding the five thousand with five loaves and two small fishes, when all mysteriously were given enough and to spare, "Gather up the fragments that remain, that nothing be lost"?

At Christmas God risks his credibility. His Son

> was in the world, and the world was made by him, and the world knew him not. He came unto his own, and his own received him not. (John 1:10-11)

And then? And then? The most momentous conjunction in Scripture, "but":

> *But* as many as received him, *to them* gave he power to become the sons of God, even to them that believe on his name.

Christmas

Midnight Mass at Saint Thomas on Christmas Eve is magical. Over three thousand worshipers cram into the church. Rugs are placed over the floors for people to sit on. Despite the crowded space, the reverence of the worship is profound.

A service of preparation for the liturgy itself begins at 10:30, where the vast congregation forms its own choir as it sings carols and prayers are said. And then the mystery of Christmas unfolds.

The
Mukluks

Some people we know are wholly predictable. They
can be counted on to react in the same way to the
same stimuli. They rise like a trout to snap the fly you
flick over them. They always have the same excuse for not
doing what you ask of them. Boring, often. Maddening,
more often. But the good side you rely on. You can count
on them, if they are punctual, to be on time. If they dress
carefully, you can assume that they won't come to your
supper table as though they had dropped in from Hawaii,
aloha shirt open to the navel.

We tend to picture God as totally predictable. A nice
old Santa Claus with a sack full of goodies. For those, at
least, who haven't offended him. White. Someone who
doesn't come over the threshold of your life until you are
ready to ask him in. The very essence of gentlemanliness,
with all of a gentleman's predictability. The supporter of
our ventures into prosperity, who smiles at affluence and
doesn't make much fuss in our ear over the less successful
than ourselves. Play the game and Santa-God will pat you
on the head—that's called a blessing—and put something
nice by way of a present into your outstretched hand.

Let me say that God is good with giving presents. But not in the way you think. Not predictable, not in the slightest. You can rely on his love but you can't hope to channel it into your life toward your pet project, whether that is yourself, your sex life, your finances, your upwardly-mobile family...whatever. Things don't work that way. You can't turn a spigot and wait for the divine generosity to flow. Things work very differently with God.

In the first place, "he gave gifts unto men"—as the Psalms say—to people who, when he gives Christ to the world, neither expect the gift, recognize the gift when it is given, *want* that particular kind of gift anyway, and are reluctant to give it house-room. God's gifts are more like a pair of genuine Eskimo mukluks (soft shoes) I was presented with in northern Canada in 1966 when I was with Archbishop Michael of Canterbury. The tanning of the leather was by a process unmentionable from the pulpit. As a result the mukluks—which were beautiful—stank to high heaven. What do you do with a gift you can't have in the house? They couldn't sit in Lambeth Palace, then my home with the Archbishop and his wife Joan. So my mukluks were given to my young nephew whose mother, my sister Anne, refused to allow them into his room and consigned them to the garage. Complaints were then heard from his father that the garage stank and the smell had got into the car seats.

God gives Christ as a surprise to the world. Hardly anybody notices. Nobody very much recognizes the gift. There was no formal presentation, no chance to prepare to receive the gift. It is, you might say, left on the doorstep and you fall over it, almost, before you notice it is there at all. And when you realize what it is, you don't welcome the gift.

How silently, how silently,
    the wondrous gift is given!
So God imparts to human hearts
    the blessings of his heaven.
No ear may hear his coming,
    but in this world of sin,
Where meek souls will receive him,
    still the dear Christ enters in.

Christ is the gift nobody has been ready for. From Day One until now. The worse thing is that he lives in those lives we have tried to avoid. The unsuitable, the indigent, the inadequate, the homeless, whose silent sitting at street corners presents us with all sorts of misgivings. He lives in people we don't want to know, because of color or sexual proclivity or misshapenness in one of a myriad of ways. Christ lives there in those lives, as well as in the eminently suitable lives that you and I have.

Or have we given him houseroom? Think! Have we said, "O come to my heart Lord Jesus, There is room in my heart for Thee?" And if not, why not? Tonight. Tonight. Now is the time to say this deep down in the center of your heart. Don't expect a predictable God to give you the Christ you picture. He is disconcertingly different. You may wish to put him in the garage of your life because he is difficult to exist with. But God's unusual gift has your name on it. And he wants you to receive him.

John, in his wondrous gospel, put it this way:

He came unto his own,
    and his own received him not.
But as many as received him,
    to them gave he power
to become the children of God....

Operation
Restore Hope

D o you remember Wednesday's photograph on the front page of the "Metro" section of the *New York Times?* I appreciate the way the man in the Saw Mill River Parkway tollbooth in Yonkers gave candy canes to the drivers as he took their money, dressed as Santa. But when you really get down to deal with Christmas you have to deal with sadness, as well as Santa; with cruelty, as well as Christmas trees; with misery, as well as mistletoe. You have to deal with them because they are the sour soil from which *a wondrous and unexpected blossom springs.*

Christmas is not the surprise of the century: it is the stupefying event of history. Stupefying because in the worst of possible times, when things have never been so bad for folks—when people are at the end of their ropes, when families stagger to recover from houses shattered by storms and from jobs blown away by the recession; when loved ones discover they are HIV-positive; when respected leaders are caught in criminal acts—when things are at the very bottom and the world is a cold and lonely place, you might, if you listen hard, hear a baby cry.

The cry is the cry of need for reassurance and love— and warmth and food and fresh clothes. It is the cry of

God: God in Christ who slipped into the world unnoticed and under the cover of night, and in through the back door of events. This is what happened on this night and at this time. It wasn't Sarajevo then with its policy of ethnic cleansing. It was the subjugated nations of Rome's empire being hit for taxes. It wasn't Somalia then. It was the spiritual famine of whose creators Christ later was to be so critical: the religious establishment of his day who laid burdens too heavy to be borne on the shoulders of God's people. But there is a sameness about it all two thousand years later, and the people who have to bear the brunt of it have always been of the same sort: the people unprotected by ramparts of wealth and power, for whom nothing has ever come easy and whose only possessions are their babies and children. The sitting targets for exploitation and extortion.

But that baby's cry is the sign of hope. Hope for us all. It is God's own Operation Restore Hope. God's initiative is something for which we are never prepared, despite repeated reminders from Christ himself to be on the alert. God has the habit of visiting us in his socks—without shoes, so to speak. He never gives us time to put our faces right to greet him, or smooth our hair, or hide our untidinesses under the sofa cushion. There never is the best time for us to meet him, and he is always different from the way we picture him to be. In a line waiting for food, not at an appearance for an Oscar award evening. Among the dispossessed and fearful, not making a triumphant arrival in a tuxedo.

It is the most perplexing, most unsatisfactory way of making himself known to us. We are always at a disadvantage, always caught out, never ready, never expecting to meet him among those sorts of people in those sets of circumstances. But he has no intention, it seems, of doing things any other way than by surprise. Why? I'll tell you why.

I suppose you might say that God is shy. The full sight of him would be too much for us; we would be overwhelmed by it. He doesn't need to impress us, to reduce us to terrified silence. He shows his love for us by fitting into our scheme of things, at the most unimaginable discomfort to himself. The ugly sisters in the story of Cinderella called for an axe to chop off toes in order to force a foot into the crystal slipper to marry the prince, all for greed. Christ cuts himself down to our size in order to fit our humanity, but for love. Saint Paul tells us that he "emptied himself." He did it, and the humanity his nature had to fit into was pockmarked and ugly with all the unfortunate things that can happen to human beings: the sadness, the cruelty, and the misery which people in this city and all over the world are going through tonight.

But, do you know something? Christ himself is the first and greatest Operation Restore Hope. And the hope is: he brings his joy into situations that look impossible, because he mysteriously appears in the middle of them. In the hands reaching out to feed hungry children, in the faces of those who are determined to negotiate peace, in the voices of protest against violence in our streets and in our schools. Wherever people overturned by events are helped to stand upright again, wherever there is restitution and restoration, that baby's cry has been making itself heard and welcomed in the human heart. And if you listen hard, you might just hear it!

Epiphany

During Epiphanytide we celebrate the Feast of the Baptism of Christ in the River Jordan. Here are two sermons for this season of the manifestation of Christ to the world.

The
Big Squeeze

y sister Anne's mother-in-law, Norah Jarman, had an extraordinary aunt. This aunt was a character. Her thought processes managed to elude her family. God knows what other people made of them, and her. I suppose she was a founding member of the space cadets. I can remember Norah Jarman recounting to me a conversation she once had with her aunt, who smoked heavily, but only those tiny, thin, cheap cigarettes known in England by their make, *Woodbines*.

"Why do you smoke that cheap little *Woodbine*?" Norah asked her.

"Because it's quite enough for one person," the aunt replied.

Norah said of the other people who heard this answer that question marks appeared out of the tops of their heads!

This feast of the baptism of Christ by John in the River Jordan is a difficult feast to understand. It has proved sufficiently puzzling to countless commentators and theologians that, as Norah would say, question marks have grown out of the tops of their heads. I have worried over this account for years. Perhaps if I approach this puzzle obliquely, tangentially, we might be afforded a clue to its meaning....

Some people will go to surprising lengths to be accepted. Social climbers will set traps for the social lions they hope to snare. They forget their families and drop their old friends. They will try to buy their way into a particular social scene. We have heard the social goings-on in early twentieth-century Newport: a newly arrived, immensely rich hopeful throwing an extravagant party— to which nobody came.

That can be matched by the good fortune of other folks eager for recognition and acceptance: "Money talks," people will say, and it usually receives an answer too: the answer "yes." You will remember that it was in this church that the tearful and intimidated Consuelo Vanderbilt was hounded up the aisle by her determined mother to meet an unenchanted young Duke of Marlborough at the altar. He had an eye on the money. Mother could already see the strawberry-leafed coronet on her broken-hearted daughter's head. It started in misery. It ended in misery. But ambition was satisfied: at least for a year or two, Mrs. Vanderbilt could claim to be mother-in-law to a duke.

Some people will go to surprising lengths to be accepted.

Would you ever have thought that Christ may be doing the same thing? You heard the account of his baptism today by John in the River Jordan. This is a new thing which John inaugurates. The Jewish nation does not contemplate the necessity for cleansing. It is clean enough. So it thinks. Baptism is for converts to the Jewish faith, not believers. So it thinks. John baptizes the followers who heard his fierce message of conviction of sin and the need to turn from it, to repent and receive the washing of cleansing, the ritual purification from the stain of wrong-doing.

And Christ goes and has it done to himself. For no reason of sin repented. There is no sin to repent. For no purification from a stain of wrongdoing. There is no wrongdoing to leave any stain. He undergoes a ceremony for which he has none of those lamentable qualifications. He doesn't fit the bill; the bill, that is, of those who have heard the fire and brimstone of John and have decided to do something about it.

Why does he do it? To be accepted?

There is a clue. Listen again to the account, this time in modern English. It may help us to grasp what is going on:

> John tried to dissuade him [from being baptized]. "Do you come to me?" he said; "I need rather to be baptized by you." Jesus replied, "Let it be so for the present; we do well to conform in this way with all that God requires." (Matthew 3:14-15)

Christ is implying that he needs to have his Heavenly Father's approval. Approval of what? God the Father requires his son's identification with fallen humanity to be total; not in its sin, its rebellious failure to reach the target of God's will and wish, but with the condition into which that consistent rebellious failure, that sin, has lowered it. God with us not at our best but *as we are* at our fallen level, not necessarily with us in our fatal capacity for rebellion against him.

You may well believe that Christ knows the "inwardness," the very deepest meaning of a phrase he is later to use in the best loved and best known of all his parables, the Good Samaritan, when he says that seeing the man half-dead on the Jericho road, the Samaritan "came where he was."

Jesus knows that his Father wishes him to come *where we are*, the superlative act of solidarity and compassion. God wants him to get to the very bottom of things, you might say. That is in fact—in sad fact—where we are, because of our fatal self-sufficiency and our stubborn independence of our Creator, Christ cannot embrace full humanity until he is at one with the lowest of us who have fallen from the place we were meant to occupy: to the bottom of the well.

Saint Paul has a curious expression—a daring expression, a dangerous expression—which is not easy to interpret: God "hath made him to be sin for us, who knew no sin" (2 Corinthians 5:21). The New English Bible clears up the language for us:

> Christ was innocent of sin, and yet for our sake God made him one with the sinfulness of men.

And when Christ is submitting to John's baptism, submitting to it against John's will, he is starting right there. He identifies himself with the human condition of fallen creatures. We sometimes loftily and patronizingly refer to an adulterous woman as a "fallen" woman. We are all fallen women, fallen men. Fallen from the place God has wished us to occupy, as sharing his spirit, capable of loving as he loves. And Christ knows that that is where he must position himself if he is to raise us.

In the second part of that risky sentence Saint Paul encapsulates this truth:

For he hath made [Christ] to be sin for us, who knew no
sin; that we might be made the righteousness of God in
him. (2 Corinthians 5:21)

Or, as the New English Bible helps us by saying:

...so that in him we might be made one with the goodness
of God himself.

People have struggled for years to place a fancier face
on the difficulty in understanding Christ's decision to
seek John's baptism, but the plain facts I have outlined
are, I submit to you, sufficient to explain it. It figures. It
ties in with Paul's understanding of Christ: his person
and his work.

Make no mistake about it: Christ's divestment of unimaginable prerequisites of his divinity in order to cut
himself down to the size of our humanity demands extraordinary qualities on his part. He acts out of certainty
about his relationship with his Heavenly Father. He is, as
the ancient Athanasian Creed declares,

Equal to the Father,
        as touching his Godhead:
and inferior to the Father,
        as touching his manhood. (Verse 33)

He acts out of certainty that he must obey the will of
his Heavenly Father. He loves his Father and will do anything for love. He risks everything for love. He "goes public." He gets into the water when his turn comes. The
people who take God seriously have already done it. He
does it, too. God affirms him and his destiny. He sees, he
perceives, that affirmation as clearly as a dove descending
from the opened heavens to alight upon him.

This story is told on this day for a very good reason. Epiphanytide is the time of God's manifestation of himself. And there he is, displaying his divinity as a human being, completely at one with all humanity in the place where it finds itself to be: *in need.*

Remember this. Remember that Christ our God displays himself in his perfection *in terms of human imperfection.* He is to be discovered in unfortunate human situations, in places and events where people are left defenseless, marginalized, chilled with cold, hurting, abandoned, and unwell. He shines through the eyes of people who do not share our advantages. And he is to be found in the vortex of failure and disappointment, frustration and defeat. He looks for us to recognize him under a thousand disguises. The love that will not let us go is content to be present with us despite our failure to notice it or our discomfort and guilt on catching sight of it.

He has taken us on for good or ill, at the greatest disadvantage to himself, in order to bring us up to where he is, that "He might dwell in us, and we, in him."

More Than You Can Handle?

G od is never satisfied with the *status quo*. He never accepts what we assume to be the settled situation. We do what we have to do. We settle for that. Humanly speaking, that is the wisest thing we can do. When we have made the best of a bad job, when we have come to terms with what the terms are for us and we get on with our lives accordingly, when we have cut our coat according to the cloth available, we wear that coat even if it is a tight fit and the sleeves are an inch too short. Better a small size than no size at all.

All of this sounds like common sense. But it is not necessarily divine wisdom. As I said before, God is never satisfied with the *status quo*. He never necessarily accepts what we assume to be the settled situation. Peter could tell you that. With nothing to show for a night's fishing, he and his partners make the best of a bad job: haul the nets to land, mend what has to be mended, wash what has to be washed, stash the nets back into the boats for another try, and hope to God the results will be more encouraging. But, sleep first; a little R & R before the next try.

Until, that is, that troublesome Jesus of Nazareth appears on the scene. He commandeers the boat, interrupts the mending and the washing, and asks to be taken a short distance from the shore. Then he sits down and uses the prow as the pulpit. Peter is the captive audience. He is the prisoner of the pulpit. Here is a man with a lot to say and he's using Peter's boat to say it; and all Peter had really wanted to do was to accept a no-catch situation and to cut his losses. It is common sense.

But it is not Christ-sense. He makes a further demand; and the request is from a carpenter, not a professional fisherman:

> "Put out into the deep water, and let down your nets for a catch." (Luke 5:4)

Peter has been there before. All night he has plied that deep water. Not a thing. He tells Christ so: "We've worked hard all night and haven't caught anything." The experience of frustration.

There *is* a place for frustration in our lives. It may surprise you to hear this. But the experience of not succeeding after hard work at a project may help us redefine our objectives, refine our methods, reexamine our motives, and possibly rediscover new avenues. We are witnessing steady and repeated frustration with tackling the AIDS virus or discovering the causes of cancer—their secrets evade thousands of research scientists, and the disappointment-ratio is heavy. But not to the extent of declaring that further efforts are hopeless. It makes us seek only the more carefully, to try even harder, against all odds.

Think about this. Is something eluding you to which you think you have a clue toward fulfillment? Even when your present experience tells you that your chances are slim?

At the risk of personal intrusion I want to tell you what I found in the city of Preston, where I worked as rector and dean twenty-three years ago. I should have applied to myself the ancient classical advice I have passed on to you from this pulpit before, Epicharmos' dictum: _Keep your head and don't forget to disbelieve._

Nothing I had been told by my enthusiastic but inaccurate bishop was as I found it to be at Preston. The rosy picture of the city and its challenges bore no relation to the realities. It was a despairing, dispirited, disappointed, dysfunctional city—full of self-pity and querulous blame-finding. City planners had had their perfect way, with the result that all the streets were one-way, and all going out of Preston. The depleted parishes snarled like hungry dogs over a bone of parochial life and initiative. Response was zero to anything new. It had all failed before. "We've worked hard all night, and haven't caught anything."

At Preston there was a disinclination to think in a new way, to imagine anything which called for a new look, a new view. The city was sleeping the sleep of death, as the Psalms say, the ultimate and tragic settling for the _status quo._ I preached my heart out. No response. I brought new people in. No response. New faces, new voices, new ideas met with indifference. It was like talking to a brick wall.

But there was one thing. Proud Preston—as the citizens called it—had celebrated a festival every twenty years, since the 1100s when King John of the Magna Carta fame was on the throne, and the church played a part in that festival. It was my luck that the festival was to be celebrated in my time. We geared our energies to the Preston

Guild, and unbelievably the frustrations and disappointments cracked apart as the city's inertia was shaken.

The town began to lift up its head. We redecorated the
dingy ancient church in colors: we put medieval blue on
the angel roof where the carved wooden angels were given
white nighties and gold wings and harps. As the pace
picked up, ideas flourished. I suggested a flower festival
in the church. The music took off. Rows broke out.
Where these is life there is disagreement.

God was not satisfied with the *status quo*. He broke our
frustration when we put out into deep water. In the face of
our experience he required us to throw out our nets where
hitherto there had been no catch.

I regard my "ministry of frustration" at Preston as an
essential prelude to the ministry he next gave me here at
Saint Thomas. I can never thank him enough for helping
me to grasp the divine concept:

"Behold, I make all things new...." (Revelation 21:5)

Now I would go so far as to ask nominees for a spiritual
office if they have had the blessing of frustration in their
previous ministry. Not only that. God has an alarming
habit of asking us, expecting us, to attempt the impossible. He trains us for it by permitting us to experience
frustration, disappointment, and even failure. You will remember that Peter and his partners, once they have put
out into deep water, take such a haul of fish that the nets
split and the boats begin to sink. God requires them to
cope with more than even they could bargain for. He gives
them the challenge of the impossible.

God does not play fair with us. Our idea of fair is that
we get what we think is our due. What God may think is
our due is often more than we can handle. If you ask me

why he does this, all I can tell you is that he wishes us to grow "unto the measure of the stature of the fulness of Christ" (Ephesians 4:13). Growth is a strain. Growth can be a pain. God accepts us not on our assessment of what we think we can handle but what in his loving wisdom he knows we can *become*, if we will let him give us what he plans.

Which is, when you think of it, why he tells Peter: you think you have more than you can handle now. Just wait! What I want you to *become* are fishers of men. I will make you fishers of men. He enables us to become the impossible thing he asks of us. Catching men for Christ is, to Peter, news from another planet. It will involve him in further frustrations, disappointments, and humiliations— not least from his challenger, Christ himself, and over Christ himself, when betrayal and denial stain him in the night of Christ's arrest in the garden of Gethsemane. Go over Peter's life and you will find it pock-marked with failures to achieve and disappointments numberless. Next to Judas Iscariot he must be the most flawed of the apostles—and this is the man Christ enables to be the Prince of the Apostles.

God is not satisfied with the *status quo* of Peter's unsatisfactory character and the frustrations and failures it produces. His over-certainty in the fishing incident we have just heard; his sudden panic when he sinks in the water having leaped from his boat to run to Christ; his misplaced humility—"You shall never wash my feet!"—and his boasting of eternal loyalty and love soon followed by his denial. His irresponsibility in cutting off the ear of the High Priest's servant in the garden-arrest of Christ. If ever there were a flawed character here is one. And the marvel is that under the impossible load of responsibilities laid upon him by his Lord he grows "into the measure of the stature of the fullness of Christ" so that he emerges as the Prince of the Apostles.

Now this can be a worrisome thing for the likes of you and me. The church is made up of failed, disappointed, and frustrated people. It has far more than it can handle in catching men and women for Christ in its task of evangelism. Its clergy are equally flawed and faulty examples of humanity. To the charge that the clergy and bishops are an inferior lot—which is true—the answer could with truth be given: we have only the laity to choose from.

When we confront our failures, limitations, and frustrations, it is difficult for us to grasp how God can allow us to experience them, yet he uses them to help us grow nearer to him if we will let him. As you know, Saint Paul was keenly aware of this truth. When he prayed that God would remove them, the Lord's decision was: "My grace is all you need; power comes to its full strength in weakness." Paul could then say,

> I shall therefore prefer to find my joy and pride in the very things that are my weakness; and then the power of Christ will come and rest upon me. (2 Corinthians 12:9)

Those are not merely words of faith. They are the testimony of experience. Paul is a man full of personality limitations: irascible, self-assured, given to express himself irritably and demandingly. Not the sort of person we would want on the vestry of Saint Thomas. God help us all.

But Paul knows the truth of this issue and he is frank enough to tell us what it is. This gives me encouragement when I consider how despite myself the work to which he has set me can get done in the lives of the people I live among; how despite my failures, profligacy, and wastings he can salvage and save "that which remains so that nothing be lost" in the tasks too great for me to tackle and too much for me to handle. He teaches me that while I must be grateful for the work his faithful accomplish for him, I must never be satisfied, for he is never satisfied with the *status quo.* God will not only allow, but will *set* limitations upon me, for his Son gives me a cross to shoulder if I wish to follow him where the going is hard and there are his sufferings to share. That same Christ, who

for the joy that was before him, endured the cross, despising the shame, and is now ascended to the right hand of the throne of God.

THE
SUNDAY
BEFORE LENT

On the Sunday before Lent begins, we try to prepare people for the fast of Ash Wednesday and the penitential season of Lent.

The

Opposite Page

It can be a bracing experience to discover what you're in for. I learned this week from a professional friend who helps me with my tax returns what my obligations will be in a few days' time when I send them in. Those obligations—discovering what I'm in for—have got my attention, as we would say. I owe more than I thought I did, or could. What is more, I shall have to do something about what I owe.

Not for nothing does this experience stand at the door of Lent. Lent can be a bracing experience to discover what you're in for. You find that you have obligations to satisfy. You find that you are expected to satisfy them, if you mean business as a Christian, if you take Christ seriously and you take your faith seriously. My first parish priest, old Father Hammersley, used to say to us individually as curates, "I've never let you down, and I'll never let you off." He kept his promise.

The curious thing is that this is precisely how God deals with us. He never lets us down, and he never lets us off. Lent is the time for that realization to be experienced. It is a bracing experience. You are required to *give*, to part with something you cherish. Something you don't think you can live without.

It can be brutally uncomfortable. As a student I saw the great state portrait of King Louis XIV. There he stands, resplendent in heavy ermine and velvet and cloth of gold, with legs in white stockings and shoes with high heels painted red, a luxuriant black-haired wig cascading curls over his shoulders and an imperious look on his face. The Sun King. You will have seen it, many of you, in books if not in full-size. It was painted to impress.

It did impress. It *does* impress. Grandeur, unimaginable wealth, limitless power, enormous dignity, majesty personified.

And then one day I opened a book and saw this portrait on one page, and a brilliant drawing based upon the portrait on the opposite page. But without the wig. Without the robes of state. Without the shoes. I saw a much smaller, bald, heavy-jowled man with a bulging paunch and pot belly: a pear shaped, unattractive, and very ordinary little person—like all of us without our pretensions, our posings, our protective clothing, and our disguising paint. And when we hear again those words of Scripture, "God looks upon the heart," we realize that we are an emperor without clothes, before God.

What you owe to God in Lent is the *will* to be open to read the opposite page, to take an honest look at it.

How much smaller are we than we like to picture ourselves? In terms of unreadiness to forgive, to kill old grudges and begin a relationship afresh? With our hesitation to be generous with what we have, and our laziness in taking initiatives to help when need of one sort or another is brought before us? With our social pretensions, our climbing, our hopes of recognition by people we long to

be among? With claiming status for our families and ourselves, real or imagined, and reminding others of our
claims? With our snobberies and our judgments in careless talk and gossip by giving the impression we are privi-
leged with information? With our assumptions of
influence and patronage, that we have the ear of the important and can get things done? With living in the past
and being unwilling to come to terms with lesser realities
and more sober circumstances? With resenting criticism
and having self-justification at the ready? With our secret
betrayals and disloyalties to those we love? All these and
many more hide the unattractive figures we reveal ourselves to be on the opposite page, before the One "unto
whom all hearts are open, all desires known, and from
whom no secrets are hid."

To make a start with all this is what Lent is about. It is
what the ashes on Ash Wednesday are about. "High and
low, rich and poor, one with another," of every color and
every background and every degree of ability and learning, we are marked alike with those ashes, for "all have
sinned and fallen short of the glory of God."

We all owe God our apology. We come on Ash Wednesday to make it. We open the book with our grand self-rep-
resentation on one side of the page, and on the opposite
page, the cruel drawing of what we really are, under all
the ermine and the velvet and the cloth of gold and the
high heels and the curly tresses of our wig. We come before him with the book open, for him and for us to see the
opposite page, and for him to help us see more closely and
more clearly by the light of his countenance the disfigure-
ment we have made of what he created "in his own image."

We make time on Ash Wednesday to do this. Of course it is inconvenient. Of course we are busy. Of course the travelling is a problem. Of course there are clients to see and meetings to attend and interviews to hold or to be given. But from 8 A.M. until 6:30 P.M. this place is open and a priest is on duty all day if you can't make either the 8 o'clock or the 12:10 or the 5:30 liturgies. If you can't manage to get here you might manage to get to someplace else. But treat Ash Wednesday's observance as a top priority, and you will be starting the process as you are meant to.

And through the Sundays of Lent we want to help you achieve what you heard Paul say in the portion we read of his epistle to the Philippians this morning. Paul had had his book open and had looked at both pages:

> If anyone thinks to base his claims on externals, I could make a stronger case for myself:...Israelite by race, of the tribe of Benjamin, a Hebrew born and bred; in my attitude to the law, a Pharisee; in pious zeal, a persecutor of the church; in legal rectitude, faultless. But all such assets I have written off because of Christ....I count it so much garbage, for the sake of gaining Christ...with no righteousness of my own, no legal rectitude....All I care for is to know Christ, to experience the power of his resurrection, and to share his sufferings, in growing conformity with his death, if only I may finally arrive at the resurrection from the dead. (Philippians 3:4-11)

There you have it, in a remarkable outburst of eloquence. Paul knows penitence. He has looked at the opposite page. He calls all the self-conscious things *garbage*. All he cares for is to know Christ, to live Christ's resurrection life, to share Christ's sufferings, and to rise with Christ.

That is what you can hope to see when you look up from examining the opposite page of your books.

This is going to be a joyful as well as a penitent time. Penitence is not alien to joy. Self-realization may cause us to be more thoughtful, but not necessarily depressed, when we look at the opposite page. Our sense of need may well develop. Our sense of purpose may well be sharpened. Our sense of duty may well be heightened.

I knew a man who had cause to turn again and again to the opposite page. An impatient man in several ways, an arrogant man in others; a snob at times, and capable of being high-handed and hasty. He was a great priest, and a penitent poet. Eric Milner-White was Dean of York Minster. He wrote a prayer for Lent, and you can make it your own prayer if you like.

> Lord, bless to me this Lent.
> Lord, let me fast most truly and profitably,
>> by feeding in prayer on thy Spirit:
>>> reveal me to myself
>> in the light of thy holiness.

> Suffer me never to think that I have
>> knowledge enough to need no teaching,
>>> wisdom enough to need no correction,
>> talents enough to need no grace,
>>> goodness enough to need no progress,
>> humility enough to need no repentance,
>>> devotion enough to need no quickening,
>> strength sufficient without thy Spirit;
> lest, standing still, I fall back for evermore.

Show me the desires that should be disciplined,
    and sloths to be slain.
Show me the omissions to be made up
    and the habits to be mended.
And behind these,
  weaken, humble, and annihilate in me
    self-will, self-righteousness, self-satisfaction,
      self-sufficiency, self-assertion, vainglory.

May my whole effort be to return to thee;
    O make it serious and sincere,
      persevering and fruitful in result,
    by the help of thy Holy Spirit
      and to thy glory,
        my Lord and my God.

Reconciliation

There are certain things in life over which we have no control. They make us sad. They make us mad. They may even make us bad. But they are there and we are here and no amount of wishful thinking will make them go away. One method of avoiding them is to go away ourselves, but often that is not possible. So we come to terms with the situation.

As I look at the scaffolding in the sanctuary to the left of the High Altar I am reminded of the time when our choir, with the choir of Winchester Cathedral, performed the world premiere of Andrew Lloyd Webber's *Requiem*. The elaborate stage structure went over the choir stalls and was made to be dismantled easily for the liturgies on the Sunday. But they had calculated without the delicate tuning of the numerous microphones placed strategically over it all, so it couldn't come down in time. We came to terms with the situation by placing a temporary altar in front; the choir occupied the staging, and the High Altar was effectively screened from view. I had to tell the surprised congregation something and so I told them that this was what Westminster Abbey looked like at the Coronation. Reconciliation with an uncontrollable event came with laughter. We came to terms with the situation.

You may not like it, but you put up with it. It could be noisy neighbors who fight and shout all the time. It could be an unfortunate marriage which you can't and perhaps shouldn't get out of. It may be an unpleasant boss or an uncongenial job, and without joining the long lists of the unemployed you have to come to terms with the situation. It may be a physical or facial disadvantage, something which causes you pain or embarrassment when you meet people. Not one of us has been freed from having to reconcile ourselves with a situation or a circumstance beyond our control. One of the simplest of these and one of the deepest is the death of somebody we love with all our heart, or the approach of death of somebody whose life is wrapped around with ours.

But reconciliation goes deeper than putting up with something you would rather not put up with in the first place.

The reconciliation we consider this Sunday is a much more costly and precious commodity. It has within its fibers the threads of forgiveness, and what Saint Paul describes as "forgetting the things that are behind" and looking to a future, "convinced of a sacred destiny in response to a sacred invitation and requirement." Looking forward into eternity, in fact. For the realm of eternity is not only God's, but God himself.

Reconciliation is a coming back together in mind and heart. When two people divide, we often describe it as a "falling out." The two separate, as far physically as circumstances will allow. We have all heard of the situation of this happening in a family under one roof. Earlier this century, in Edwardian times, a lady holding a great social position in Britain took a lover. She derided her husband in letters to her lover. Her husband perhaps didn't have the imagination to know what was going on behind his back until somehow her letters fell into his hands. Her cruel remarks of betrayal, disparagement, and infidelity almost killed him. From that day he never spoke to his wife except in public when guests came to their famous house. When he was dying she sent a note begging him to allow her to come to see him in his part of that great house. He refused, and died unreconciled.

It is easy for us to be arm-chair critics. Why didn't they talk it out? Why didn't she own up and ask his forgiveness for the children's sake? Why didn't they find some way—as most of us would have tried—to face, confess, receive forgiveness, and forget the things that were behind? It is not necessarily our business to question here, some ninety years later, in another age and in another country. But that tragedy's name is Legion, and it is going strong to this very day: silence and separation within the privacy of house-walls, maintained unrelentingly and unremittingly.

The way back after falling out can be very hard. With two people, the move to separate the relationship is made by both, though not necessarily at the same speed and to the same distance. But with God it is different. People have written and testified about a distancing they experience from God. When this happens, when a soul feels God is far away from its concerns and anxieties and insecurities, it is that soul who has moved away, not God, whose love is constant and unrestrained and in no manner diminished and eternally available. "Thou art the same...."

Reconciliation then between God and us must always be a one-way street. We come back to God. His readiness to reconcile has been the experience of his children from the dawn of the experience of him. In the prophecy of Jeremiah is that remarkable statement of God's readiness to reconcile—not with an individual so much as with a nation of individuals:

> "I will make a new covenant with the house of Israel and the house of Judah, not like the covenant...which they broke, though I was their husband, says the Lord....For I will forgive their iniquity, and I will remember their sin no more." (Jeremiah 31:31-34)

There it is. The divine forgetting. The readiness to forget in the act of God's acceptance of his people's desire for reconciliation. God is prepared to wipe the slate completely clean. But you have to come back to him to have that slate wiped clean.

Christ himself exemplifies this. Saint Paul's extraordinary insight into the role of Christ among us could declare that "God was in Christ, reconciling the world unto himself" (2 Corinthians 5:19). Paul has just taken a fresh dip of ink for his pen after writing:

> When anyone is united to Christ, there is a new world; the old order has gone, and a new order has already begun. From first to last this has been the work of God. He has reconciled us men to himself through Christ. (2 Corinthians 5:17-18)

This last sentence puts, in a nutshell, the plan and purpose of God for his Son, who himself could say,

> "I shall draw all men to myself, when I am lifted up from the earth." (John 12:33)

Reconciliation with God through Christ could only be effected through Christ's terrible death on Calvary. That is the cost of it all. And that is one of the benefits of his Passion.

The author of the epistle to the Ephesians puts it like this:

> He destined us…to be accepted as his children through Jesus Christ.…For in Christ our release is secured and our sins are forgiven through the shedding of his blood. (Ephesians 1:5-7)

But the situation doesn't end there, as if we were somehow lifted off the hook to live happily ever after, reconciled with him. For God "has entrusted us with the message of reconciliation" (2 Corinthians 5:19). Paul hits the nail on the head twice with the hammer. He adds:

> We come therefore as Christ's ambassadors. It is as if God were appealing to you through us: in Christ's name, we implore you, be reconciled to God! (2 Corinthians 5:20)

We are meant to use the benefits of Christ's Passion to bring others to the knowledge of this "amazing grace," as the hymn describes it.

I have taken pains to go at length through this theological thicket with you as we look toward the season of reconciliation the church calls Lent. Reconciliation isn't complicated so much as basic to our understanding of what God is about in his dealings with us. It can be expressed in five moves, so to speak—

1. God's love for us is unalterable;
2. Our love for God is alterable at best; we alter our course, we move away from him;
3. Christ's task to us is to draw us back to him;
4. It takes terrible suffering, culminating in the cross;
5. Reconciliation to God involves bringing others to the knowledge of it.

This last practical consideration is a challenge all of us have to face. In the first place you can't preach it without practicing it. This bitter truth the church has had to learn, to its shame. People outside the church, non-believers, take one look at the divisions within the church through history—the arguments, the fights, the martyrdoms, the cruelties, the consignments to hell, the separations, and the condemnations—and say, "If the churches can't get their act together to be reconciled, how can they preach a gospel of reconciliation which bears the stamp of integrity?" Our divisions and separations have caused a scandal and a stumbling block to an unbelieving world. That is a profound embarrassment to what we lightly call Christendom.

Localize it. Individualize it. Personalize it. Now is the time. If we have been involved in any separation and sundering of a relationship, the cause of Christ is hampered until somehow that division is healed, and we have done our very best to assist the healing process. It is not easy. Bruises stay for a long time. We all know that we are responsible for the impression we create upon other people. If we give the impression of being generous-hearted and accepting and conciliatory, and that impression is genuine, then after a time others will feel drawn to be accepted and reconciled, and healing will under God take place.

We allow the love of God to do its perfect work. Remember that there are no family relationships, no personal relationships, no parishes, and no political parties which are immune from the bruises of division and difference, and upsets and rows occur in the best and regulated organizations among people who are trying their best. This happens. People get hurt and progress and achievement are harmed by the hurt. The task of the Christian is

to climb from under the wreckage and seek for opportunities to set things in right perspective again.

Who is equal to these things? That is a fine rhetorical
question from the Bible itself. The answer?

I can do all things through Christ who strengthens me!
(Philippians 4:13)

ASH WEDNESDAY

These three brief Ash Wednesday sermons were delivered at the 12:10 liturgy. At this service the church is packed to the doors, and it takes six of us to administer the ashes at the front of the chancel steps.

Be Prepared
to Sweat

You have probably heard a woman on the television say the title of this sermon: *Be Prepared to Sweat*—an ad for a robust exercise regime, which, they tell us, "ain't no dancin' class." Lent ain't no dancin' class, either. It is hard work. We need that hard work. Take a look in that unsparing mirror with the light of truth full on and see the traces of the fat of laziness and uncaring; the sagging areas of self-indulgence and self-pleasing; the wrinkles of self-concern that have spread like a map over the soul; the aging of compromise with this world's superficial standards and swift judgments and prejudices. The reflection is that of somebody who has let himself go.

Today is the day to enroll. The aim is reclamation, renewal, revitalization, restabilization, the reduction of accumulated fat around the thighs and stomach of our procrastination and our capitulation to standards less than the honorable, the accommodations we make with ourselves and others as we settle for "what's in it for me?"

The first thing to do is to strip down. We let things go that we rely on and think we can't do without. There's a wide range of excuses: for unpunctuality and for not repaying what we owe; for failures to fulfill our obligations to the work we are paid to do and to the people in our lives. Let us strip off the excuse-layer we have tailored for ourselves. Think for a minute. Just where is your self-excusing worn with effect? What are the areas in your daily routine where you can strip down?

Forget the bit about doing without sugar in your coffee. That isn't an act of penitent self-denial: it merely spoils a decent cup of coffee. Go deeper. Hit where it hurts. The pocket. If it will help you, I will tell you of a surprising calculation I made that hurts. My parish family all know that I am partial to vodka martinis. Two good ones in an evening. Say they cost five dollars each in a restaurant. Multiply that by six for the week. That's sixty dollars. Five weeks of Lent; that's three hundred. Send a check for $300 to the Choir School Mobile Kitchen for the poor and homeless. Now I *can't* afford those martinis, and some folks will eat.

To what purpose? We owe it to God. We need to say sorry to our loving Creator for letting ourselves go. We are here to receive the token of our regret for being so outrageously self-centered. The ashes are a sign of that penitence. The church reminds us with them that all we selfishly accumulate is in the end worthless, like the cinders on our foreheads. Good for nothing. For the love of Christ alone we need to be reduced to size, so that we can develop the muscle he wants for our lives to be "lived unto God," for time and for eternity.

We have heard the bad news. The good news is that you are here because you are prepared to sweat. And you are cheerful as well as penitent. The Lord loves a cheerful giver. Give yourselves to this Lent, for love of him, so that you will be within touching distance of him and hear his whispered words of encouragement as he works you over.

Forgiveness from the Heart

Some of us find it impossible to forgive. We nurture the memory of an injury, pamper it, nourish it until that memory is strong enough to have a life of its own. It follows us around like a great black hound, silently dogging our tracks, always there and always making its presence felt. It puts its cold nose into our hand to remind us to pet it, pat its head, or assure it of its place in our lives. It is always hungry, always pleading to be fed. We feed it when we ought to let it starve. We cherish it when we ought really to give it no house-room at all.

Harboring a grudge, nurturing the memory of an injury, may give us the perverse strength to go on. Collectively we see it in our streets and nations and the wreckage it creates for everybody. Individually we see it and the disintegration it brings to the personality and powers of judgment within the soul which will not let that memory die. It is an unpleasant neurosis.

Christ has some unpleasant news for those who will not forgive and forget. And Ash Wednesday, when we come to apologize to God for the wreckage we have made of our own lives and of others', is the time to remember that God's forgiveness is not automatic upon an Ash Wednesday appearance. Especially if we ourselves are holding a grudge or a sense of injury which we are not willing to concede, hand over, and leave to God.

The hiding place is the heart. A heart that harbors an injury is known in the Scriptures as *hard*. Ash Wednesday is of all days the time when we are made aware of the importance of the heart, the seat of our emotions and will, the fountain of all our generosities, the source of all our affections, and the cesspool of all our hatreds and revenge. It is where heaven is experienced, and hell is entered.

You are here today for a short time. You have the chance to go back onto Fifth Avenue a different person. A new person. With a new heart. Think as you sit here of who it is who has hurt you, injured you, caused you grief. Then think (if you can imagine the enormity of it) of the damage you have done to God's love, and the wounds your unwillingness to forgive has caused in Christ's sacred heart of love. Know that you cannot leave here forgiven unless you make an act of forgiveness now. Now. If you've made it you can claim Christ's forgiveness for yourself, because you have obeyed the Scripture:

> Rend your heart and not your garments
> and return to the Lord your God.

Do you want to be the person you hoped to be? The person God designed you to become? A new person back on Fifth Avenue? With a new heart? When going down those steps you can say to yourself that sentence from the Psalms:

> This is the day which the Lord hath made:
> I will rejoice and be glad in it.

This may indeed be the first day of your new life.

The
U-Turn

Colombian coffee ads on the television have capti-
vated me for years. Remember the Simplon Express train screeching to a halt and backing into the
tunnel for Paris, where the coffee had not been loaded?
But it is the great jet plane in a clear blue sky doing a perfect U-turn to retrieve the coffee for its passengers that
speaks a parable to me. It tells me a parable of our journey
through life, perhaps under skies not so cloudless or so
blue, not so direct and sure of its direction. The realization suddenly comes that the substance which gives life
its flavor and its zest has, through neglect, not been
brought on the journey, and that the life of the present
and the future will not be the same without it. The decision is made to turn. To turn back, and start again with it.

Ash Wednesday is the day of the U-turn. *Metanoia*. Repentance. Get back to where you left that precious and
life-enhancing possession to reclaim it, and travel with it.
That possession is a *presence*. Christ's companionship. You
were given access to it, you were given a right to it, at
your baptism. You were made heirs, coheirs with Christ,
as the Bible says, to an inheritance. What is his, is yours.
Make no mistake. What is his, is yours. And you have

either through neglect or through distraction with what you think are more important and more relevant things in your life risked the loss of your inheritance.

You will be familiar with the Jacob and Esau saga. I was listening to it being read last week at Morning Prayer before Mass. Jacob was a skunk. He cheated his brother of his inheritance. We all know that. It was inexcusable. We feel sorry for Esau. But Esau had thought so lightly of his inheritance and its responsibilities that his neglect invited advantage being taken of him. Jacob took it, and the inheritance, too.

We all stand at risk of losing that thing that gives life its savor, its speed, its purpose, and its rest, if we neglect to cherish and make our own the gifts of our inheritance.

You know this. That is why you are here. It is the day for the U-turn. Ashes on your head after your prayers of apology are the outward and visible sign of an inward and spiritual turning. This is not the day for good resolutions. New Year's good resolutions are as tough as wet newspaper now.

Today is when you say sorry. To God. You reach for your inheritance, Christ's companionship. His hand is ready for yours to hold. There is the uphill climb to Easter through his cross, with the struggle and the pain and some loneliness too, and out into the sunshine of the resurrection.

You need to say another prayer. A prayer of gratitude that you got up this morning and *didn't* smell the coffee, and came here for a fresh taste.

LENT

The weeks of Lent through Palm Sunday provide a strategic opportunity for concentrated Christian teaching. Over the years our Lenten sermon courses have ranged over the topics of theology, moral issues, and the Christian life.

Included here are four sermons from a course I called "Seven Denials: The Best At Risk," which was based upon the seven occasions of denial found in the Lenten readings from Saint John's gospel.

Humility
at Risk

"You shall never wash my feet!" (John 13:8)

F or over a fifth of a century in our time together
here at Saint Thomas, you have been taking Lent
seriously. You have come in the hundreds—thousands, to
be more accurate—on Ash Wednesdays to apologize to
God and to receive the ashes. You have listened carefully
to over twenty Lenten sermon courses preached; you have
tried (at least) to make some observance of self-denial
during these weeks every year. And you have been an encouragement and an inspiration to the priests who try to
look after you and draw their support from your ready
and generous response to all the things we ask of you.

Lent is as good a time for praise as for penitence, and I
want you to know how appreciative we are for what you
do to affirm our ministry and priesthood among you.
Tackling Lent's demands, as a family; hearing things said
frankly, as a family; facing requirements for the extra effort and the extra mile, as a family; and finally arriving at
Easter's gates after the poignant Holy Week and Passion
of Christ, all together as a family, has helped individuals—like my sister Anne, for instance—to grasp what a

community of faith can be and can do, and to be converted by it, as she was, here in this place.

Using your head as well as your heart is the purpose of our Lenten sermon course. I discovered while reading the chapters of Saint John's gospel, recording the last days and hours of our Lord's ministry in Galilee, that there are seven intriguing occasions of *denial*. A denial is registered and it places at risk some precious quality in the human heart and personality. Those best things that I have identified are: humility, integrity, truth, justice, theology, credibility, and faith.

They are aspects of our character: what we do because of what we believe and hold dear. To be humble, upright, truthful, fair, honest to God, believable, and believing are precious qualities in the human soul. Putting even one of those qualities at risk is a dangerous business for that soul, involving compromise with the lesser good, or even throwing in your lot with evil. It is, in very truth, playing with fire.

The people around Christ in the gospels are playing with fire. Take Peter, the least satisfactory and least promising of Christ's disciples. He is volatile, emotional, unstable. His heart often rules his head. His mouth outruns his heart at times. One could wish at this stage that Peter might pray more and say less. As it is, he is saying too much. We all know people who have Peter's disease. They will never quit while they are ahead.

People have talked their way out of jobs. They have talked themselves into impossible situations. The Bible speaks of the tongue as an undisciplined limb. Saint James can write very tellingly:

Think of ships: large they may be, yet even when driven by strong gales they can be directed by a tiny rudder on whatever course the helmsman chooses. So with the tongue. It is a small member but it can make huge claims. What an immense stack of timber can be set ablaze by the tiniest spark! And the tongue is in effect a fire....No man can subdue the tongue. (James 3:4-8)

In case you think James is going on a bit, I have news for you. He devotes two-thirds of the third chapter of his letter just to this. And it is more than possible that James would know Peter and his talkative ways.

Where was it that Peter could say anything so rash? Let me tell you. During the Last Supper, Jesus gets up from the table and takes his top clothes off. He takes a towel and ties it around him; like a slave he pours water into a basin and begins to wash his disciples' feet and to wipe them with the towel. Saint John then records:

When it was Simon Peter's turn, Peter said to him, "You, Lord, washing my feet?" Jesus replied, "You do not understand now what I am doing, but one day you will." Peter said, "I will never let you wash my feet." (John 13:6-8)

Strange it is how pride and self-sufficiency can camouflage themselves as humility even to the proud and self-sufficient soul. Luke tells us that an unseemly row had broken out shortly before this, when the disciples jostled for precedence and prestige. They have with them their teacher, and they display bad manners in arguing in front of him as to who was Number 1 on the team. It is only a supposition on my part, but I doubt that Peter had stayed silent in this row. Could you imagine Peter as a shrinking violet in that ruckus? My guess is that with his temper he comes into the ring fighting and everybody hears plenty from him.

Silently Christ takes hold of the situation by stripping down to do the job a servant would normally do. They had all sat down to the table with unwashed feet because nobody would pick up the bowl and put water in it to do the job. They had argued that it was beneath them; each pointing his thumb and curling his lip at the next, until there was nobody left to pick on.

From what John says it sounds as if Peter is somehow interrupted and surprised by Christ. "What, Lord? *You,* wash *my* feet?" Probably he has been talking so much that he had not noticed what Christ was doing. And Christ responds, "You do not understand now what I am doing, but one day you will."

Peter makes a big mistake. He thinks it is beneath Jesus' dignity and he says so. What Peter fails to realize is that humility doesn't necessarily involve being willing to do a menial task. Humility involves accepting the service of someone you don't think should offer it. Can I help you? No, thank you. I don't need *your* help, at any rate. That is pride. The deeper test of humility is agreeing to be helped from an unsuitable source.

Humility at risk. At risk from a subtle source. Not agreeing to accept the help of another. Not welcoming the approach of someone offering service to you. It was Archbishop Michael Ramsey who used to point out to young priests, in his instruction to them about to hear the private confessions of people, that confession was allowing Christ to stoop at their feet in order to wash them and make them clean again; that the deepest test of humility was to *allow* Christ to perform the servant's role for them.

Self-sufficiency of a certain kind can be a curse. Early
in my time here, a man and woman started attending the
liturgies. Paul is a professor at a nearby university. Tim-
mie, his wife, is a highly intelligent and learned woman.
Children were born to them and we watched as a family
began, and rejoiced with them. Paul had been what he described as a secularized psychologist whose conversion to
the faith involved, as he said, "a collapse of [his] secular
ideals accompanied by a quietly growing change of heart
and mind."

He wrote a book in which this church and our ministry
to him and his family were mentioned fondly and gener-
ously, called *Psychology as Religion: The Cult of Self-Worship*. In it Paul applied his keen critical faculties to the
subject that had enthralled him and to the views he would
no longer consent to teach. He had come to hate selfism,
the notion that we are, in the words of the Prayer Book
collect, "sufficient of ourselves to help ourselves." He
talks at one point in the book about "the beauty of dependency, on how to find humility."[1]

Did you notice the conjunction of the two: dependency
and humility? Dependency is a dirty word for us. It con-
jures up pictures of drugs and alcohol. But there is a holy
dependency and this is part and parcel of the humility
Christ longs to see in us. Not a dependency on people:

> Put not your trust in princes, nor in any child of man: for
> there is no help in them. (Psalm 146:3)

---

1   Paul C. Vitz, *Psychology as Religion: The Cult of Self-Worship* (Grand Rapids,
    Mich.: Eerdmans Publishing, 1977), 12, 129.

Certainly not dependency upon yourself. Dependency on God. Not merely on what he will *give* you, but on the ways he can *serve* you. And what are those ways? The sacraments are some, where he can cleanse you and feed you and strengthen you and impart his joy and his strength to "comfort and restore" you. The readiness to give him access to you, to allow him to come in and clean house for you is an aspect of humility on your part, and a reflection of his. Other people can be another way to learn dependency on God: "Christ in friend and stranger," as the Saint Patrick's Breastplate hymn puts it.

Lent is a time for realizing that he can serve you in situations you would not choose, at the hands of people you would not choose, whose motives you may suspect or despise. You may not welcome this fact or this way of learning humility, but you may be sure of one thing: God has a habit of allowing us to learn humility by being humiliated. It is in fact one sure way he has with us in the lessons he wishes us to learn about this. Don't ask God for humility unless you are prepared to be humiliated. If you are not prepared for the likelihood of the scald of shame and humiliation, don't ask God to help you to be humble.

We learn the lessons in situations in life that we don't orchestrate. They are not like a piano lesson, where you are given a set piece to learn by practicing, and then perform for your teacher. There are the notes. There is the piano. There is the piano stool. You flex your fingers and start. God's lessons are the sort where you have something put in front of you which is unthinkable, never for a moment imagined, for which you have had no experience to recognize, nor time to practice and make perfect. Confronted with it, you are at a loss.

That is the secret. You have nothing of your own to fall back upon to help you recover your poise or control of the situation. You emerge the loser, it seems, having been at a loss. You leave the situation smaller than you thought you were, reduced by it. And being helped in a way you deem inappropriate from a source which surprises you by its unsuitability is a lesson in humility. And it is God who motivates that unsuitable source to help you grow in humility.

Did you see that delicious film *Driving Miss Daisy*? How Jessica Tandy as the old lady was affronted by having a driver drive her car for her, so she rejected his help and spurned his service to her? Do you remember how, little by little, her humility grew from her humiliation at being considered no longer competent, until in the end her driver was her best and most beloved friend?

Integrity at Risk

"I am not!" (John 18:25)

Y ou would agree with me that if among us today there are visitors to Saint Thomas we should do things to help them feel at home. The ushers will have seen that they have their leaflets and their seats for the liturgy. I must see that they are brought up to date with the course of sermons we have embarked upon this Lent.

The sermons in this course are aimed at being of cumulative value, building one upon another as we consider seven denials from Saint John's account of the last days and hours of our Lord's ministry before his crucifixion. These denials are by different people, and each denial places at risk a precious quality of one sort or another in a human soul. They could jeopardize the chances of that soul to function clearly.

Last week we heard a denial from Peter that put Peter's humility at risk. He refused to let Christ wash his feet. Refusal to accept help from a source you don't approve of puts humility at risk.

This week we are listening again to Peter. He is in the courtyard of the High Priest's house. He has been allowed in because we think that young John (the disciple whom Jesus loved, you remember) might well be a member of that High Priest's family and thus has right of entry, taking Peter with him into the house.

It is the night of the arrest in the Gethsemane garden. The garden is a favored place for Christ to take his disciples. I remember that garden from a visit there in 1966, where I said my prayers on an April night with Archbishop Michael Ramsey. The olive trees in the garden give shade in the sun, and they also make the place darker at night. As they gather in this accustomed place Judas takes the Temple police and a posse of soldiers by prior arrangement to the entrance. Jesus comes out to meet them and asks for whom they are looking. Jesus of Nazareth, they respond. In Peter's hearing Christ gives an answer of special significance: the phrase by which God in the Old Testament had revealed himself to the Israelites. He says, "I Am." Not only Peter but the Temple police and every Jew within earshot knows those words instinctively as God declaring himself. I Am. Note this. Note this and remember it.

Jesus is taken. Peter pulls out his knife and in the melée slashes at Malchus, the High Priest's servant, and severs his ear. Peter is, as we saw last week, emotional and unstable. Christ is bundled off to the High Priest's house; the adrenalin is running in Peter, who follows him, possibly with young John. Certainly the companion is admitted by the woman at the door, and when she asks Peter, "Aren't you also one of the disciples?"—expecting the answer "yes"—Peter's adrenalin turns to water.

When you think of it, it must have taken a lot of adrenalin to get Peter from the garden into the most dangerous place in Jerusalem. Put yourself in his shoes. If you had pulled a knife on the Cardinal's secretary, could you see yourself knocking on the door of the Cardinal's home? And what would you say in answer to the maid's question?

Saint John makes a point of recording Peter's failure to acknowledge his membership: *"I am not."* I AM. I AM NOT. The divine self-revelation. The coward's denial.

Around the charcoal fire lit to keep themselves warm this chilly night, Peter then joins the Temple police and the staff of the house, to share the warmth. He is spotted and is asked again the question put to him by the woman at the door: "Aren't you also one of his disciples?"

No fire on earth can warm Peter's courage. He miserably says *"I am not."* And then a relation of Malchus, whose ear Peter had severed, insisted, "But I saw you myself, didn't I, with him in the garden? I saw you!" Total defeat for Peter's integrity: *"No; I am not."*

Integrity at risk. Go back to the Last Supper, where Peter had said too much too soon. He had jeopardized his understanding of humility in denying Christ the opportunity to serve him by washing his feet. There had then been the scene of the first desertion, when Judas after a cryptic remark from Christ had slipped away from the supper table and the room and into the night. Peter had asked, "Lord, where are you going?", and Jesus had given him almost exactly the same curious answer as at the feet washing, where he had said, "You do not understand now what I am doing, but one day you will" (John 13:7). He now gives this answer, strangely similar:

> "Where I am going you cannot follow me now, but one day you will." (John 13:36)

To which Peter finds himself saying,

"Lord, why cannot I follow you now? I will lay down my
life for you." (John 13:37)

Big words. Big promises. Big claims. Big deal. Those
curious and mysterious answers of Christ challenge both
important and precious qualities in Peter's soul: humility
and integrity. After all that fine talk about self-sacrifice—
"I will lay down my life for you"—now comes self-saving,
self-preservation.

Integrity comes from the Latin word *integer,* which
means "together." Integrity means having it all together,
having a character in which strengths of varying power
form a pattern of wholeness. It is an inner honesty. It has
nothing to do with being pleasant, still less to do with being charming. Both David the fornicating and adulterous
king and Peter himself have charm. Immediacy of character in the case of both of them is a component of charm.
Integrity has something of the quality of bronze in it: a
hard metal, and a beautiful one, also, like steel. You can
have a cutting edge with both. And both can have reflecting surfaces, so that you can see yourself. So integrity has
both an inviting quality and a warning quality. You can be
drawn to it and you can be put off by it. You can admire it
and you can be repelled by it.

The hard side of our Lord's integrity is shown in the
fact that crowds of those who were attracted to his teaching left him because what he was saying was too hard for
them to be comfortable with. They could not take it. It
cut them to the heart. It cost them too much. When he
spoke of self-sacrifice, they thought of self-preservation.
They moved away from him after being attracted to him.
Perhaps their consciences would smite them after they

had done so. Perhaps they could feel guilty: their own integrity at risk.

Integrity demands that you admit your allegiance, and take the consequences of that allegiance. During the persecution of the Christians in the time of Nero and the pagan Roman emperors, a simple question was put to Christ's followers: Have you been baptized and thus claim Christ as Lord and God? That was all, we are told, that they were asked. Upon saying yes, the sentence immediately was returned. Death. It meant death to admit your allegiance. Would you think it fair to guess how big the church membership in this city, or even in this church would be if the same circumstances were to exist and the same question were to be asked?

Integrity demands that you admit your allegiance morally as well as religiously and spiritually. As a Christian the temptation to avoid the incursion of the state into our affairs is with all of us. We all resent paying high taxes. We all hope against hope that we won't be audited. Why do we hope we won't be audited? Would we be caught in an evasion of sorts, a reliance upon a loophole in the law that doesn't in fact pertain to us? The very term "tax shelter" places the integrity of Christians at risk before the eyes of him who warns us to "render unto Caesar the things that are Caesar's and unto God the things that are God's."

Denying responsibility places our integrity at risk. As a parent we have responsibility for our family's well-being. As an employee we have responsibility toward those who pay us what we earn from them. As an employer we have responsibility for the lives of those we employ, their welfare, their safety, their prospects, and their morale. As a citizen we have more than fiscal responsibility toward our community. "No man is an island, entire unto himself." For some of us the responsibilities we shoulder are part of the cross Christ expects us to carry as we follow him, with his. We can no more duck our responsibilities than we can hope to persuade another person to shoulder our cross for us. Ducking them is denying them. Denying them can destroy our integrity.

The term "NIMBY"—Not In My Backyard—is one with which most of us are familiar. We have seen communities unwilling to have a hospice for AIDS patients along their street. I received some years ago a letter of complaint from a neighbor living next door to us in the Museum Tower about the homeless around our church whose presence disturbed him on Fifty-third Street. It gave the place a bad name, he said. Somebody's personal integrity was being tarnished by self-concern.

Integrity demands that you admit your allegiance. That allegiance may be to your wife or husband, to whom promises have been solemnly made and with whom you have an undertaking to be true and faithful. Your integrity is on the line when you stray outside those vows for something different, perhaps something younger, something more exciting, perhaps when you say "I am not" to yourself when the question arises as to whether you consider yourself bound by those vows.

I am always incredulous when people who desire public positions of responsibility and trust are found unfaithful to their vows and declare their guilt in terms of merely a "mistake." People with integrity can make mistakes. A mistake is a genuine failure to discern a correct strategy or word, or a true choice. With a lot of men who wear the same make of raincoat, a mistake frequently occurs at meetings or on the coat rack. I have done it, and it has

been done to me. But you know what your husband or
your wife looks like. And to find yourself going off with
somebody else isn't a "mistake." It is a collapse of integrity. It is a sin. To plead this sin a "mistake" does further
damage to integrity.

And when in fact I lower the standards of priesthood
by failures to keep my temper or to show generosity of
spirit or to receive others with the doors of my heart fully
open, I know that I am refusing to admit my allegiance to
Christ. Aren't you also one of his disciples? And I find
myself saying *"I am not!"* And the integrity of my priesthood is compromised and threatened.

Those assaults upon our integrity come from all sides.
And Christ, whose temptations in the desert were in truth
to compromise his integrity as the Son of God and to admit his allegiance, knows only too keenly how strong they
may be. The Scriptures tell us that he was tempted in all
ways as we are, yet did not sin. Our task is in fact our
hope and our salvation: we look to Jesus and the oneness
he had with his Father, and the power of his redeeming
death and resurrection, to bind us back together.

Justice
at Risk

"For my part I find no case against him." (John 19:6)

Sermon writing is a tricky business. After thirty-seven years of it I should know. But I have news for you. It doesn't get easier; it can, if anything, get harder. It is humiliating to realize how often inspiration eludes you. Occasionally a flash-point for a sermon explodes to get the thing started. Flash-points are rare. I once heard a well-known preacher announce how the title and subject of his sermon sped into the quadrangle of his Oxford college, painted on the side of a van delivering flowers: "Wreaths and Crosses Made to Order." He was able to make the point that you can't have the cross Christ gives you to carry made to fit your shape and comfort. Christ sees to that for you.

Something of the sort happened this past Tuesday when a chilling article revealed that an international and independent court of inquiry had found that the murder of Jesuits in Salvador some years ago had been sanctioned by the Top Brass in that country. The President of Salvador was understood to have encouraged the country in a broadcast to sweep this appalling miscarriage of justice under the rug and to award its perpetrators a blanket pardon. Justice is very much at risk in Salvador.

Justice at risk. We are considering seven occasions in Saint John's narrative of the last days and hours of Christ's ministry before his crucifixion when a denial was uttered that could jeopardize, impair, and put at risk a quality precious to the human soul for its balance and health. We have considered two so far: humility and integrity. Today we hear a denial which puts justice at risk, for a subtle and surprising reason.

Jesus has been arrested and taken first to the house of Caiaphas, where Peter has tried to save his own skin by denying that he is a disciple. It is early in the morning now and Christ is taken to the governor's headquarters: from religious territory to the secular arm of the military force. Pontius Pilate has an uncomfortable posting. He is sitting on top of a powder keg: holding down by force a resentful, seething, occupied territory at a time when its occupants are preparing to observe a national religious holiday.

We all know what heat and anger the observance of an ethnic holiday can produce. Some of you are aware that my views of the antics of leaders and participants concerning the Saint Patrick's Day Parade last Wednesday aren't necessarily complimentary. Interest groups raise issues that others would prefer not to be raised; arguments become shrill and accusations fly. People resort to the loathsome practice of imputing motive.

Jerusalem is a beehive dangerously close to careless, kicking feet. Overturn it and many people will be stung. It is all set for an observation that asserts its ethnicity, that raises its religious consciousness, that brings its claims about God and itself defiantly into the sunlight, in the face of its pagan conquerors. It is possible that at no other time in the year is the temperature so high in rebelliousness.

The place is crammed with pilgrim-tourists, a security risk for a start. People have gathered from far distances to retell and reenact their ancient deliverance from a pagan conqueror. There are layers of triumphalism between resentment, scorn for the pagan army of occupation concentrated upon its commander, the unfortunate Pontius Pilate. If you read the narrative carefully, without overstating the case, you might be right in concluding that the governor, Pilate, is a nervous wreck.

He has been in trouble before, we are told. Things have gone wrong under his command. Complaints have reached Rome. Rome has been displeased. There is a sense of insecurity and unease about this man. The Scriptures describe in this way the part he was obliged to play in an incident he would prefer to avoid, for the dangers of disgrace and deposition are real:

> From Caiaphas Jesus was led into the Governor's headquarters. It was now early morning, and the Jews themselves stayed outside the headquarters to avoid defilement, so that they could eat the Passover meal. So Pilate went out to them and asked, "What charge do you bring against this man?"
>
> "If he were not a criminal," they replied, "we should not have brought him before you." Pilate said, "Take him away and try him by your own law." The Jews answered, "We are not allowed to put any man to death." Thus they ensured the fulfilment of the words by which Jesus had indicated the manner of his death.
>
> Pilate then went back into his headquarters and sum-

moned Jesus. "Are you the king of the Jews?" he asked.
Jesus said, "Is that your own idea, or have others suggested it to you?" "What! am I a Jew?" said Pilate. "Your
own nation and their chief priests have brought you before me. What have you done?"

Jesus replied, "My kingdom does not belong to this
world. If it did, my followers would be fighting to save me
from arrest by the Jews. My kingly authority comes from
elsewhere."

"You are a king, then?" said Pilate. Jesus answered,
"'King' is your word. My task is to bear witness to the
truth. For this was I born; for this I came into the world,
and all who are not deaf to truth listen to my voice."

Pilate said, "What is truth?", and with those words
went out again to the Jews. "For my part," he said, "I find
no case against him." (John 18:28-38)

I want you to spot a clue in the telling of the arrival at
the governor's headquarters. The Jews escorting Christ
from the High Priest's house refuse to step over the
threshold. The feast of the Passover is a few hours away
and the Law says that they will be defiled if they tread on
pagan, godless territory. Strange it is that people can be
involved in cruelty and vengeance and cloak it under
spirituality. At one and the same time they are knowingly
framing an innocent man, they are concerned with the
technicalities of religious purity. At least, on the surface
they are. They know and we know that *that* ritual defilement could be washed away by a bath before dusk. But
they choose not to tell Pilate so, and instead protest
loudly in front of him a puzzling, infuriating, religious le-
gality.

So loud indeed that he makes a tactical error. He gets up and goes out to them. He concedes. He loses his position of advantage.

They see him coming. No amount of imperial swagger will cover his error; no peremptory remarks can hide the fact that they are calling the game. He could well have known two things. He could have known that their protest against defilement is hollow, and he could have known that his refusal to appear on their terms would have put the ball right back into their court, and in their court they are forbidden by Rome to execute a man. His refusal could have been dangerous for his career: either cowardice or irresponsibility. Hazarding a guess in history from the pulpit is as dangerous as speculating theology from the pulpit, but isn't it possible that self-concern on Pontius Pilate's part could have unseated him momentarily? And in that momentary *dislodgement* a man's life could be placed on the wrong side of the balance?

It seems from the evidence we have that Pilate is the unfortunate, unwitting, unwilling, and unclever individual allowed by God's permissive will to find a place center stage of the created world's history. He is not the only man in a plight like this. I well remember a classmate of mine from seminary who found himself appointed dean of one of the famous cathedrals in the world: Salisbury. No sooner had the excitement cooled and the smoke dispersed than he found he had a crippling capital campaign to mount and to manage for the famous spire. It would cost several millions of pounds. He was totally unprepared, totally unschooled for an assignment of this magnitude. The work he had thought he had been brought in for was there all right, and there was plenty of it. But it paled beside the urgency and the enormity of the sum he was expected to achieve from an England mired in recession and financial famine. "I didn't sign up for this..." he said to me in despair.

Nor had Pontius Pilate. He could have had no inkling of his fate to be mentioned day by day ever since when the creed is recited in the liturgy said in a myriad of churches throughout the world, and to be regarded with disdain and hatred by souls who hardly know his place in history.

Pilate goes back in to question the prisoner accused of being an habitual criminal. He soon finds himself out of his depth. It is an uncomfortable interview, and John the narrator writes the conversation carefully. Pilate cuts the interview short and leaves the prisoner to tell the authorities outside:

> "For my part, I find no case against him."

Pontius Pilate's *denial*. He wants no more part in a situation over which he has lost control. He wants to be free of a responsibility which embarrasses him. And so he puts justice at risk.

Of the great concepts of human behavior and achievement in the Scriptures, justice looms very large in importance. Never for a moment imagine that the people of God treated this achievement lightly. To them, God stood as the epitome and fount of all justice; justice is an aspect of God's love. It is part of his character. The psalmist can sing:

> Justice and judgment
> > are the habitation of thy throne;
> mercy and truth shall go
> > before thy face. (Psalm 89:14)

In the psalmist's mind mercy and truth are components of that divine justice. It is strange indeed that Pilate had just asked oratorically, "What is truth?" before leaving his prisoner, Christ, to tell the leaders who had arrested him that he wants no more part in the prosecution of this case. Along with mercy and truth as components of the divine quality of justice goes something else: the divine quality of *judgment,* and we hear the injunction in Isaiah:

> Keep ye judgment, and do justice: for my salvation is near
> to come, and my righteousness to be revealed. (Isaiah 56:1)

The way that some of our contemporary New York religious leaders speak, you would think that the issues of social justice were a discovery made by them and their gurus within the past thirty years and brought to light and life in the sixties. I have news for them. Amos the herdsman from Tekoa was thundering his denunciations of the exploiters of the poor and the marginalized from the deserts in the days of King Uzziah: he scolds Israel with the promise of divine wrath those who

> sold the righteous for silver, and the poor for a pair of
> shoes...and turn aside the way of the meek. (Amos 2:6-7)

I have gone to some length to sketch for you how supremely important the concept of justice is to Israel's understanding of the personality of God, and how the people of God are required by their Creator to wield God's justice among his men and women, reflecting his respect for their individuality, all made in his image. Embodied in this concept of mercy and truth supplying the fibers of divine justice is *the necessity for a sense of responsibility.* You can't check out from this responsibility by denying involvement, especially for self-concerned reasons.

How often do we read of people who fear to supply evidence in a court of law because of possible or imagined reprisals? Haven't we witnessed cases in which people on the street will stand aside as violence against someone occurs, for fear of being involved? People can witness an act of injustice and say "I saw nothing." They haven't seen it because they will not face their responsibility of witnessing to the truth. It happens around us on our streets all the time. I know that their distaste for involvement may be based in nasty reality. I know, for instance, how terrified people can become in the drug scene and the violence which erupts and which could reach them and their families—and has—in the attempts of the law to bring the perpetrators to justice. It is a very complex issue, but beneath all the elements there is the wish to be free of involvement: "for my part I find no case against him."

This morning we can thank God for a man we do not know except for his face flickering on the television screen: General Morillon, the French commander of the United Nations forces in the Serbian conflict. Many times the trucks bringing in food and medical supplies to save the lives of those choking to a death of famine have been stopped by Serbian paramilitary gunfire. Finally, the general himself assumed personal responsibility in this flagrant act of merciless injustice and got into his car to lead the way. He reached the starving inhabitants, set up his headquarters, and began relief operations on that very site. One small act of real courage and compassion in a welter of flagrant injustice.

Isn't General Morillon simply and perhaps unconsciously doing what his Lord and ours did? Like the good Samaritan of old, he refused to walk on the other side of the road. Instead, *he came* where we are.

Credibility
at Risk

"My kingdom does not belong to this world." (John 18:36)

I want first to commend all the brave and committed souls who have stayed with this sermon course through Lent. This is the sixth Sunday of considering a series of denials recorded by John in the narrative of the last days and hours of Christ's ministry before his crucifixion, and after. Today, John records a denial from Christ himself, inside the governor's house. It is a dangerous denial. Let me read the setting for it from Saint John's gospel:

> Pilate then went back into his headquarters and summoned Jesus. "Are you the king of the Jews?" he asked. Jesus said, "Is that your own idea, or have others suggested it to you?"
>
> "What! am I a Jew?" said Pilate. "Your own nation and their chief priests have brought you before me. What have you done?"
>
> Jesus replied, "My kingdom does not belong to this world. If it did, my followers would be fighting to save me from arrest by the Jews. My kingly authority comes from elsewhere."

"You are a king, then?" said Pilate. Jesus answered,
"'King' is your word. My task is to bear witness to the
truth. For this was I born; for this I came into the world,
and all who are not deaf to truth listen to my voice."
(John 18:33-37)

Much has happened to Jesus in the hours following the
first Palm Sunday. Listen to John describing that event:

The next day the great body of pilgrims who had come to
the festival, hearing that Jesus was on the way to Jerusalem, took palm branches and went out to meet him,
shouting, "Hosanna! Blessings on him who comes in the
name of the Lord! God bless the king of Israel!"

Jesus found a donkey and mounted it, in accordance
with the text of Scripture: "Fear no more, daughter of
Zion; see, your king is coming, mounted on an ass's colt."

At the time his disciples did not understand this, but
after Jesus had been glorified they remembered that this
had been written about him, and that this had happened
to him. The people who were present when he called Lazarus out of the tomb and raised him from the dead told
what they had seen and heard. That is why the crowd
went to meet him; they had heard of this sign that he had
performed. The Pharisees said to one another, "You see
you are doing no good at all; why, all the world has gone
after him!" (John 12:12-19)

You cannot hear these words without realizing that this
is the acclamation of a king from the crowds who had
gathered. Make no mistake. It wasn't simply a few disciples around the seated Christ slowly appearing on a donkey: this is a sea of people. Why? I'll tell you why. John
describes them as a "great body of pilgrims" (John 12:12).

A good Jew observed these obligatory festivals: Passover, Pentecost, and the Feast of Tabernacles. Jews traveled from all over the earth to be in Jerusalem if they could possibly get there for the Passover. To this day Jews in countries great distances away have a greeting to each other as Passover approaches: "This year, here; next year, in Jerusalem!" The great ambition for a Jew, like for a Muslim to visit Mecca, is to be in Jerusalem to celebrate the Passover.

Lambs are slain at the Passover. It is part of the rite. A census taken revealed that 256,000 lambs were sacrificed that year. Multiply that number by a family per lamb, to put a conservative estimate on it, and you will have a multiple of a million pilgrims pouring into that place for the observance. It is an astonishing number to contemplate cramming into that small walled city.

A sea of people converges on Jesus. They have heard that he has raised Lazarus from the dead. Imagine the effect that that could still have today. Jesus is experiencing what we New Yorkers would call a Wall Street ticker-tape parade as he comes in; the cry goes up, "God save the King"—the ancient welcome and acclamation.

You would expect him—everybody then would expect him—to be astride a horse, mounted on a war-charger. He rides a donkey. A horse is a warrior-king's mount. A donkey symbolizes peace. "King of glory, King of peace!" It is the prophesied sign of the Messiah. An ocean of faces crowd around his procession. Palms are waved. The noise is deafening. The Pharisees are frantic: "You see you are doing no good at all; why, the whole world has gone after him!" They have seen it all and they know.

This is not a protest demonstration. This is an international as well as a national recognition and welcome of a king on his way to his coronation. The parallels we have in our contemporary lives with that first Palm Sunday are strikingly similar. The Pharisees are only too aware that this is not an eccentric happening, a few friends clowning their way into the festival. The Roman army on the alert for national disturbances within their occupied territory of Pilate's province of Judea are only too aware that this is no isolated incident of ethnic enthusiasm.

Pilate evidently has received some sort of report about this when Christ is brought to the governor's headquarters after his arrest and summoned into his presence.

"Are you the king of the Jews?" (John 18:33)

He may have heard the noise of the welcome himself. The answer he gets is both a yes and a no. Christ talks about his kingly authority *as possessing it*. Yes: he acknowledges his kingship. No: he disclaims royal territory. "My kingdom does not belong to this world." Sovereign territory is not asserted. At a geographical level, at least.

"If it did [belong to this world], my followers would be fighting to save me from arrest by the Jews. My kingly authority comes from elsewhere." (John 18:36)

It is the "elsewhere" that defeats Pilate. Sovereignty implies territory, temporal power. And Christ denies any claim to this. Incredible! Here we have a man, albeit a mysterious person of authority, putting his credibility at risk by a denial.

Not that this is a new experience for Christ. As John in the prologue of his gospel wrote so poignantly,

He was in the world, and the world was made by him, and
the world knew him not. He came unto his own, and his
own received him not. (John 1:10-11)

That is the key that is struck at the outset of John's account. We know what we are in for, so far as our measure
of the success of his ministry among humanity could be
made. His own refused to take him seriously. His own
people simply would not believe him. And doesn't Christ
himself tell us that a prophet is not without honor, except
in his own territory? The gospels refer to Christ's failure
to accomplish any great work with certain groups "because of their unbelief"—that is, because his credibility
was disregarded. You have only to look at the unhelpful
attitude of his own family. We are told that they found
him and his claims embarrassing and insupportable.

All through his ministry Christ has found his credibility questioned. The Pharisees continually have questioned it. And now this. At the very end his denial to
entertain territorial claims while maintaining his kingship opens him up to contemptuous disbelief.

It happened then and it has happened ever since to
those who own him as Lord and God. Saint Paul can write
about this very thing—our credibility at risk—when he
says in his second letter to the church in Corinth:

As God's servants, we try to recommend ourselves in all
circumstances....Honour and dishonour, praise and
blame, are alike our lot: we are the impostors who speak
the truth. (2 Corinthians 6:4, 8)

He is saying that as Christians our credibility is at risk
when we proclaim the Christ as our Lord and God who

denies worldly kingship. We have to be prepared to be
tarred with the same brush by a disbelieving world.

The world does disbelieve Christ's claims. How many
of your own family don't even bother to give them a try?
How many are prepared to accept those claims *only on
their own terms*? How many of your own family regard you
as slightly odd for professing your Christian beliefs? Start
there, and widen the circle of your acquaintances. Your
colleagues at work look at you; they look at your professed beliefs. They look to see if your faith makes a difference to your life. If it does, there is puzzlement as to
why you should bother with a scheme of things many
think is irrelevant to modern existence. Being impostors
who speak the truth isn't always a comfortable profession
if your faith makes a difference to your life.

And what if it doesn't? What if the beliefs you are
known to profess simply fail to make any difference at all
to your lifestyle and your behavior? If people know you to
be a practicing Christian and nothing of your faith shows
in the way you deal with yourself and others, can they be
blamed for disbelieving? If you refuse to forgive; if you
continue to hate; if you demand vengeance; if you spread
hurt and injury through unkind gossip; if you cheat on
your partner or steal somebody else's; if you are stingy; if
you are dishonest? Not only your credibility but Christ's
credibility will be at risk, when folks discern that who
you say you worship and what you say you believe seem to
make absolutely no difference to you, whatsoever.

A diplomat and Oxford professor, a Hindu called Sar-
vapelli Rhadakrishnan, once scathingly said that the
Christians he had met were for the most part very ordinary people making extraordinary claims. There was little, if anything, to substantiate those claims when you

looked at the lives of those who professed them; they were uninspired, no different from the lives of people who didn't make those claims. They were, he said, unaffected by what they claimed they worshiped. And the Hindu simply could not come to terms with that. The lives of the people who shared his religious beliefs were profoundly affected by them. They were distinctive. *They could not help being distinctive.* Enough said....

You will remember those disciples around Christ whose lives left much to be desired. They got under his feet, most of the time. What they *were* impeded his credibility, until the resurrection and Pentecost bathed a new light upon their souls and brought a new fire into their hearts. Then you will remember how people on seeing and hearing them discerned Christ alive in them, and believed and were baptized. This credibility was apparent or became so, and souls were won because of it.

In the drama of this coming week we watch as Christ's suffering kingship sustains all attacks upon it, all denigrations of it. What was written in irony on the placard over his head nailed to the cross, along with his hands and feet, has become our tattoo, our brand-mark: Jesus Christ, King of the Jews. To Pilate, a jest. To us, a recognition, a rebuke, and a saving reminder.

MAUNDY THURSDAY

The ceremonies on the evening of Maundy Thursday—the washing of feet, the procession of the Blessed Sacrament to its "grave" in the "garden," the stripping of the altars, and the sudden departure in flight—are cumulatively moving events. These three homilies are sparse, for if ever actions speak louder than words, the Maundy Thursday ceremonies so speak.

Drying
Our Toes

W hen Paul writes "love never ends," he is writing about Christ. For the love that never fails
and falters, never comes to the end of the tracks, is also
the love for us that carries Christ through this hideous
evening of treachery and betrayal, desertion and abandon-
ment to the forces of darkness, to the loneliness of the
cross tomorrow and on through death tomorrow after-
noon. By saying little, Christ's action in stripping to perform the slave-duty of cleaning people's feet, in fact, says
everything: Nothing is of importance to God in matters of
his own majesty and dignity as he displays the humility of
his love.

He loves not from a height but from below our heads,
beneath *our* dignity. His love gets onto the ground to express itself to us. This is why we so often fail to notice his
loving us. Our heads are in the clouds of self-preoccupa-
tion, self-preservation, self-service. We never look down
to where it is all happening because we are looking up for
the next opportunity to get something for ourselves, if
necessary before somebody next to us has had the chance
to notice. We are out for ourselves. Meanwhile from the
earth-level—the word humility comes directly from *hu-*

mus, earth—the love of Christ washes our feet in forgiveness, for, like the soldiers who will hurt him so tomorrow when they hammer his hands to the wood, we know not what we do.

This is the night when all that Christ teaches us of God's inexplicable patience and preoccupation with us is put into a silent scene: with God, naked, at our feet, gently drying our toes after we have trampled over everything he has made and loved.

The
Bittersweet
of Betrayal

There is a bittersweet taste about this liturgy. You will have witnessed the nobility of the feet-washing, of our bishop kneeling to wash the feet of twelve people just as Christ took the towel and girded himself to perform the slave's task for his companions, to quell the quarrel they had begun as to who was the greatest.

Count on your fingers. Twelve disciples. Twelve includes Judas Iscariot. Christ washes Judas' foot before the Last Supper begins. Judas starts his meal cleansed and forgiven by Christ before he finishes the treachery he has begun. He has made a deal. He has sold Christ already. The sum has been agreed upon. He will collect his money later. But Christ's forgiveness in his feet-washing not only covers what Judas has arranged, but the kiss of betrayal later that dark night. The divine forgiveness—notice this—isn't conditional or compartmentalized by penitence as we would assume. The generous love of God staggers the imagination. It covers not merely the commission of treachery but the *intention*.

It is hard to understand, much less to forgive, betrayal. Betrayal has many times ended in the death of the betrayer. Salman Rushdie goes in fear of his life for having betrayed the sort of Muslim faith the fundamentalist extremists want by writing *Satanic Verses*. If not death, then small pity for the betrayer. Pollard, the American who spied for Israel, has had his plea for a reduction in his life-sentence abruptly turned down. I have no doubt that the Ames couple will pay dearly for their betrayal not merely of America but of the Russian secret agents they sent to their deaths.

Tonight is the night on which Christ is betrayed. Heartlessly, cynically, for a sum barely enough to buy a plot of waste ground. You may remember those terrible words of the psalmist:

> Yea, mine own familiar friend, in whom I trusted,
> *who did eat of my bread,*
> hath lifted up his heel against me. (Psalm 41:9)

You know for sure that Christ has those words engraved on his hands, as the Bible says, when they reach into the dish to pick the choice morsel for Judas. He bears his betrayer no enmity: the traitor is symbolically forgiven as his feet were washed. Instead, Christ tells him to do quickly what he has to do.

No resentment. No self-pity. No pleading. No upbraiding. Just submission to a betrayer's kiss, and a look from a broken heart.

Trampled Underfoot

When Christ tonight at the supper table tells Judas, "Do quickly what you have to do," he is making a private appeal of love at betrayal. Christ has favored Iscariot with a gift from the plate, a favored morsel, a token of affection and regard. Arabs still do this at feasts. They offer a favored guest a choice piece of lamb from the joint in front of them. I have watched this. Judas not only gets the favored piece from the host: he *is* the favored guest, reclining next to Christ. Judas takes and eats the mark of friendship and recognition. John makes a point of saying that *at that moment* Satan entered into Judas.

Note this. Isn't it extraordinary that a human heart can be offered and can take a kindness from God, a personal blessing meant for that heart alone, a gift of encouragement for its growth into "the measure of the stature of the fulness of Christ," as Paul describes it, and yet that very gift can be the dynamic for evil?

No, it isn't extraordinary. If often happens. The gift of mathematical genius can be used to cause havoc with computer networks. And has, in the hands of young students who invade the system with a virus, wrecking people's patient work and squandering thousands of hours of expertise. A gifted painter can fake old Masters: in the fifties a remarkable artist fooled the world's experts with faked Vermeers, and made illegal millions of dollars. Fine surgeons performed the cruellest experiments on babies in Nazi concentration camps. These are callous betrayals of the affection God has for such folk.

The human heart is an uncertain vessel for the divine gifts. Maundy Thursday night can tell us this. But it tells us also that the divine love can withstand the betrayals of its generosity, the callous wastage of its gifts, the spiritual affront to its affections. And Christ, caught in the trap of betrayal by someone he loves, can say when Judas had gone out, "Now the Son of Man is glorified, and in him God is glorified...."

GOOD
FRIDAY

It has long been the church's practice to preach the seven words of our Savior on the cross on Good Friday. These two sermons consider the fifth and sixth words, "I Thirst" and "It is Finished."

"I Thirst"

We have an expression here in America about the temptation to commit something grossly improper or inappropriate. We say, "Don't even *think* about doing that!" It is an attitude we often come across when we ponder the ways of God; why he does what he does, if he is what he says he is. We encounter taboos in what is deemed appropriate thoughts about who God is: don't even *think* about seeing God in those terms.

One of the taboos about God is to imagine his *vulnerability*. I well remember, as an Oxford undergraduate in 1951 in my first year of theology, being required to study the Thirty-Nine Articles of the Church of England, that historical document of 1571 made law under Queen Elizabeth I, which is still printed in the Book of Common Prayer and to which all the clergy of the Church of England have to make an oath of assent. The very first article, "Of Faith in the Holy Trinity," begins:

> There is but one living and true God, everlasting, without body, parts, or passions....

The latter word in Latin is *impassibilis,* incapable of suffering. To speak therefore of God's *vulnerability*—that he is able to be wounded—is something we have to take a risk over with this firm assertion in Article I. But we must take a risk. If God is love, as the Scriptures put it, he is vulnerable, because love is vulnerable, capable of being wounded. He takes the suffering of humanity, whom he loves, to himself. He cannot help that. He suffers with us and ours in the name of the Father.

Today, the day we call Good Friday, Christ is on the cross, true God and true man. He cries out about his thirst. Christ is suffering. He is displaying divine vulnerability to the pain of his tortured body imprisoned by nails and motionless, fixed on a cross.

The very idea of God, who keeps everything in the universe in motion, kept motionless, nailed to a piece of wood, victim of human brutality and sensible to its agonies, disturbs me deeply. How can God submit to it? Love moves him to submit to this fearful punishment and violence. And when I hear him give voice to his suffering—admit it, reveal his need—I am surprised to the depths of my soul. It is, when you dare to think about it, one of the greatest surprises in creation. It is pretty nearly unthinkable. God restricted; God telling the pain of his thirst.

Thirst is one of the most terrible of tortures. It maddens, it causes hallucinations. The desperate search for water to slake the thirst isolates a person from rationality.

"I thirst." This sense of deprivation, isolation, which suffering of any and every kind brings with it, is experienced by Christ as part of the experience of being human. "Nothing that is human is alien to me," the ancient saying goes.

Look at him. He had suffered the pain of social isolation. People heard him say what he had to say—and left. It is a crushing experience to be rejected, either for what you are or for what you represent. I was discussing with a man for whom I have affection and respect the decay endemic in our democratic system of government: elected representatives know in their conscience which way to vote and fail to do so for fear of a disappointing showing at the next election. Upholding truth, defending a principle, wearing at times the uncomfortable mantle of the prophet, is far from the easiest way to make friends or influence people. Never have I seen a man feel so alone in his suffering for having spoken out as Archbishop Michael Ramsey did when Rhodesia unilaterally declared her independence of Britain and all Britain, it seemed, arose in wrath at his response. What he said was too hard for many to take, and some politicians saved their skins by letting him say it.

Christ spoke and was deserted by the people who could not take him for the hardness of his words, who could not face the sacrifice involved. A wall of opposition began to arise. The Pharisees had their presuppositions weighed in the balance and were found wanting. The Sadducees had their easy assumptions examined, and that was clearly *not done*; they were surprised, offended, angered, and discomfited, and they finally conspired with the Pharisees toward his downfall. He was isolated from them all.

He preached in the synagogue and the elders threw him out. Rejection. He tried to heal and in one place failed "because of their unbelief." Rejection. There was a time in his ministry when in his spiritual loneliness he exclaimed, "the Son of man has no place to lay his head." He was dismayed and made to suffer by the crass stupidity he met in the twelve he had gathered around him: vying for status, misunderstanding his role, being rough with the people who flocked to him.

And then to the week of his Passion and to the keenest suffering of all: it begins with isolation from his most trusted friends. The gospels make a special point of this.

He had made a point of asking them to pray through the night with him on the Mount of Olives in the Gethsemane garden and had taken the men who had witnessed his transfiguration, Peter and James and John, apart to do just that. He had gone forward a little, the Scriptures say, had thrown himself on a great flat rock in the garden and had gone through such a terrible experience of spiritual grief and loneliness at the reality of what his life's purpose was to cost that sweat like blood, we are told, fell from him.

> "Father, if it be thy will, take this cup away from me. Yet not my will but thine be done." (Luke 22:42)

There was nobody who could share *that*.

Luke then tells us that "an angel from heaven bringing him strength" appeared to him. But not his closest friends. There is no friendly arm, no embrace, no whispered word of comfort to him, no wiping of tears or sweat from his face from them. As if to emphasize the isolation his suffering is causing him, Christ discovers them all fast asleep, dead to the world, dead to his grief, dead to his deepest human need. There is to be nobody, there is to be nothing that might come between Christ and the suffering, nothing between him and the dregs of the chalice his Father had handed to him.

He wakes them. The soldiers come—and his disciples flee. Helter-skelter for their lives, ducking through the olive trees in the dark garden, down the slope, jumping into the Kedron brook at the bottom, back up into the crowded anonymity of a city at festival time. "They forsook him and fled."

It had to be so. Part of the cost of his suffering was to be his isolation, of which the bitter dregs was the withdrawal of his awareness of companionship with the Father, the experience which could shake the one claim which makes sense of all his others: "The Father and I are one." From the cross as he hangs there, he has shouted,

"My God, my God, why has *thou* forsaken me?"

Nobody there. Not even God. *That* is suffering: the *thirst* unquenched for companionship, reassurance, nearness. And in loving obedience he is submitting himself to this situation, in the name of the Father. Humanly speaking, it is unthinkable: a suffering God.

Today we have a notion of a planet in pain. The earth has absorbed untold pints of blood from the millions who have been cut down in cruelty; from disease, from war, for revenge; from the obliteration of a nation, now given the antiseptic name of ethnic cleansing. The perpetrators of indiscriminate carnage of one particular race can always find reasons which satisfy blood-lust or sadism. Along with you, I am outraged at the attempts thrust at us to deny the existence of Nazi atrocities in the death camps of Europe, to make us doubt the truth, to suggest that it was all a figment of the imagination.

On Monday night I was horrified to catch a part of the damning film on the eruption of AIDS: *And the Band Played On.* How human vanity and fear combined could look at facts and stifle them under personal considerations, collectively and individually not wanting to know, are sinister traits and strategies symptomatic of human selfishness still. You can lead a horse to water, but you cannot make it drink. True. True also, that for dark reasons a humans soul can flatly deny it has seen something standing stark in front of it, deny that it was there at all, or deny that it had the shape it had.

We can persuade ourselves about almost anything. Not least, human suffering. I have seen a man get angry at the mention of starvation in poorer countries of our world, as if it was an intrusion (which it was) upon his dinner-table conversation. There is in Holy Scripture a brutally graphic expression, "To shut up the bowels of mercy and compassion." It describes pity-constipation, to put it bluntly. People become inured to suffering. *The New York Times* more than once has drawn attention to people's attitude to the homeless, the inadequate, and the indigent. What were once alarm and concern have sunk to indifference and resentment. And that has reached me, too. When I hurry past a bundle of rags with a voice pleading for help and a hand outstretched, when I tell myself that to give is not the path to solution, am I shutting up the bowels of compassion? I suppose you ask yourselves this same question.

When I am bombarded with begging letters and outstretched hands asking my help; when my stomach is turned by the suffering caused by tornadoes or floods or explosions or riots; when the scalding hate in our streets and our world spill over the television screen and the pages of the press; when this scream of human suffering nearly deafens me, where do I look for answers? Where do I *go* to look?

I go to Calvary. I look at the Christ who hangs there helplessly, calling out his need. The Christ in whom all the suffering and the tears of terror and grief and bereavement, all the disease and all the catalogue of human disaster are to be found in his wounded heart of love. The mystery is too terrible to plumb. The well of suffering within him is too deep.

The divine vulnerability is an ocean of uncharted depth, a universe of unmeasured capability to suffer, and in so doing, to draw all suffering souls to himself, in the name of the Father.

"It is Finished"

When Pilate scored a cheap point against his Jewish critics who complained at the notice he had painted and nailed to Christ's cross—"The King of the Jews"—by saying, "What I have written, I have written," he thought he had finished the argument. When he had reached for the water to wash his hands of responsibility for the fate of Jesus, he thought he had finished the case. He had not finished. In both events he had evaded the issue. But he hadn't finished.

When Judas threw himself over the gorge of the Hinnom and was found dangling at the end of the rope that had strangled him, he had planned to finish it all. But he hadn't finished. His life was interrupted by violent death, but it wasn't finished.

To finish something is entirely different. There is an orchestration of events: a beginning, an accomplishment, a climax, and a tidying away: like winter succeeding the seasons of spring and summer and autumn. Like a concerto with the movements coalescing into a great piece of music.

God knows how to finish. The legend of Creation tells you so, that at the end of every day God beheld all that he had made and "he saw that it was very good." Creation was achieved.

Christ sees his time on earth as no sentimental gesture to humanity, no question of "putting in an appearance" only to disappear again into the safe comfort of the heavenly realms. His name is not Emmanuel—"God with us"—for nothing.

> "My Father has never yet ceased his work, and I am working too." (John 5:17)

His life is his work, and the work given to him to do, work gladly accepted by him to perform and to perfect, is that we "may have life and have it more abundantly." His is a working partnership with his beloved Father in the world God loves so much; to reconcile humanity to its Creator, to restore, *re*create, to make all things new.

> "What the Father does, the Son does. For the Father loves the Son and shows him all his works, and will show greater yet, to fill you with wonder. As the Father raises the dead and gives them life, so the Son gives life to men." (John 5:19-21)

There, bluntly and briefly, is the scope of the work of Christ. This is his *raison d'être*. This is his story and this is his song: his work is "in the name of the Father," and for his Father.

> "The Son can do nothing by himself; he does only what he sees the Father doing." (John 5:19)

What he sees the Father doing is maintaining the creation of the world, caring for it, caressing it, loving it with the love that "makes the world go 'round."

For him it means laying not only his reputation on the line, but his own life as forfeit, if you like, a pledge, for that is what it will take to finish the work.

And from his cross he declares it to be finished. He offers his finished work, his achievement, to the Father. In doing this he shows us two things: how to worship, and where to find joy.

He presents the perfect sacrifice: himself, without spot or blemish, totally and unreservedly set aside for God the Father, dedicated to him. Everything he is and all that he does is gladly and obediently poured out as an offering, sealed with his life-blood on the cross where, through no fault of his own, he is made to die. That oblation, that self-giving, is perfect and sufficient. Nothing can question its integrity of motive or its effective power. It is "the one true, pure, immortal sacrifice." It is the finest act of worship the world could ever witness.

And Christ in offering it gives us an example and a *way*. All we can do is to plead his sacrifice to the Father, and this the people of God have done ever since, when bread is broken and wine is drunk in memory of him: in cathedrals and upon glorious altars, in the ancient parish churches over Christendom, upon tables and rocks, secretly for fear of persecution, whispered or sung with choirs as in this place. In majesty, in utter plainness, in celebration, and by every conceivable sort of forgiven sinner as death approaches, Christ's offering of himself is remembered before his Father. It is remembered in his name through the power of the Holy Spirit, which is the Christian community's power to claim and plead and offer and share in and wonder at and treasure and long for—until the next time.

"It is finished" is his way of showing us how to worship. And where to find joy. It always comes as a surprise to us to realize that it is here on the cross and not, say, in the wedding at Cana that sure and certain source for joy is to

be reached. Christ's sacred heart has been broken, and there, at its deepest depths, is his joy at achieving all the Father has sent him to do: to ransom, heal, restore, and forgive, to "renew the face of the earth."

Do you recall this extraordinary remark by Jesus recorded by Saint John?

"A woman in labour is in pain because her time is come; but when the child is born she forgets the anguish in her joy that a man has been born into the world." (John 16:21)

The pain is still there, but pain is not alien to joy. With accomplishment, with achievement, with creation, *with giving life,* the pain of it, the agonizing hours, shine with joy; joy takes over.

Do not imagine that pleasure and joy are the same thing, or even claim the same root. Pleasure comes from within our humanity; we are conscious, and we register our consciousness of the pleasure we experience. We salivate over the prospect of some good taste, we smack our lips and grunt over some good meal, we comment our approval at some good sentiment, we moan in sexual ecstasy, we roll our eyes at the memory of some gratification. We are aware of ourselves or some part of our bodies as a pleasure comes to us and takes hold of our attention, then.

Not that this is harmful or base in and of itself, for God has made us to enjoy ourselves and things and people and situations. Having fun is not beyond his plan and purpose for us. For he has made this world funny and enjoyable both—with a myriad of beauties in earth and sea and sky, and we, as rational beings, are capable not merely of discovering these enjoyments but of identifying them, listing them according to priorities of one sort or another, and preferring some to others. We are, throughout, aware of ourselves.

With joy it is different. The hymn talks about being "lost in wonder, love, and praise." The "lostness" is the secret. Self-consciousness of any sort falls away. We are not aware of ourselves or our specific, personal human reaction. We are not so much consumed as transformed. No; better—transfigured! Something from beyond us happens that is so extraordinary, so powerful, that it changes us, briefly, into another person. The "visage of our countenance" is altered, for it is in a new light, and it hears a new music, music not of this world, but of the orchestra of heaven. Heaven, indeed, for only heaven can transfigure us, only the divine light can shine from within us, which is what happens when joy is bestowed upon us. We become another self, for all we have learned in life's school—all sophistication, all knowledge, all the tumble of events which have molded our individual psychologies and personalities and shaped our reactions—fall away in irrelevance as the soul grows, "from glory to glory advancing."

This transfiguration, even for a moment, is immeasurably strengthening. The soul is given new life, *divine* life, and because this is so, there floods a tide of new energy to communicate itself. God's personality of love naturally reaches out to make itself known. Joy is infectious. Others can see it and it can be communicated.

The transfiguration leaves its mark permanently on the soul, a hallmark of integrity, of utter purity. The lives of all the saints, I guess, are "powdered," as the language of heraldry puts it, with these marks; they form a pattern on their souls. In some way, in some deeply mysterious way, we, like Paul, could call them "The marks of the Lord Jesus." The quality of this joy cannot be measured as pleasure is measured, in terms of intensity or in length of duration. Nor can it necessarily be compared with other experiences of it like pleasure can. For the divine light which shines through the soul transfiguring it is never stronger or more piercing one moment than the next; the warmth of that flame is never easier to bear, for joy is an experience at once excruciating and unique.

But perhaps the greatest mystery about it all is its capacity of *surprise*. You never know when joy will erupt, like a sleeping volcano. There is no ideal setting for joy, no way in which with certainty it could be calculated to show itself—quite the opposite. For the most part, it will irradiate a heart broken by grief; it will shine from pain and desperate sickness; it will crown a noble love nobly expressed and unselfishly received. Joy has been known to come in exhaustion, in exhilaration, in defeat and in deep gratitude. Forgiveness will usher it in, self-sacrifice will cause it to appear. In imprisonment, in the marriage bed, in worship unself-consciously and carefully prepared and offered, in the face of danger, in the notes of music and in silence, in the spoken words of a loving soul when there is nothing left and when there is everything to live for, joy's transfiguring light will pierce an unexpected moment, and time catches its breath, for the strength of the pull of the divine love and life are felt. "He drew me with bands of love," as the Scriptures say, and heaven and earth are joined in a single peace.

This is at the heart of the encounter with God, when the frail and fettered thing that is the human soul is infused with the life of God and becomes whole and eager in its strength for further encounter and integration; when its humanness and creatureliness are regarded as of lesser

importance but assume their right stature and dignity as
the soul enjoys "the freedom of the children of God" to be
itself, the responding and responsive object of love of its
Creator.

This is the gift and its secret source bequeathed to us as
he hangs there and declares with a loud cry, "It is finished." It is perfected: it is achieved, for God. The world,
for God.

> Glorious, more glorious is the crown
>   Of him that brought salvation down
> By meekness, called thy Son;
>
> Thou that stupendous truth believed,
>   And now the matchless deed's achieved,
> Determined, dared, and done.
>
> —*Christopher Smart, 1722-1771*

EASTER EVE

The glorious liturgy of the Great Vigil of Easter, with the lighting of the new fire and the lessons telling the story of human creation, fall, and redemption, speaks for itself, and these sermons are brief.

On Easter Eve the sermon follows the part of the liturgy we call at Saint Thomas the "Holy Noise," in which, after the Litany of the Saints, the priest turns to the people in the darkened church and with open arms shouts, "Christ is Risen!" The people respond, "The Lord is risen indeed!" and the organ thunders, the choirsters ring their handbells furiously, and we all begin singing the hymn "Christ the Lord is Risen Today." It is stunning. The lights go on all over the church, and Easter begins....

The
Big Bang

There is a threat in the sound of thunder. People hear it and look up. They fear the lightning which accompanies it. It is a force too powerful to tackle. It can strike too close for comfort. But thunder as it reverberates through the heavens and echoes from far away in the air brings the sound of mysterious warfare. The ancients thought of it as the gods at battle, as the sky darkened with it.

Tonight there is a welcome thunder. You heard the organist make what the church calls the "Holy Noise." Scripture tells us that the resurrection of Christ was of such power that

> there was a violent earthquake; an angel of the Lord descended from heaven; he came to the stone and rolled it away, and sat himself down on it. (Matthew 28:2)

The crash of the resurrection. This is no gentle romantic tale of tip-toeing through the tulips to find a smiling Christ half-hidden in the cherry blossoms. This is the account of God's direct intervention in the world he had created.

The course of normal events is interrupted and the interruption is terrifying. Christ walks in his resurrection life from the tomb whose seal has been smashed and whose imprisoning door has been violently blown away. "At the sight of him," says Matthew, "the guards shook with fear and lay like the dead" (28:4). For Christ's face shines like lightning and his garments are as white as snow. God's thunder, God's lightning.

This is the strength of the power that made the world in the first place: scientists call it the Big Bang. The resurrection is no echo of the first Big Bang. It is the louder thunder of resurrection life, new life in the face of all evidence to the contrary, in the person who tells all who love him that he makes "all things new."

God is mightily at work. Those women friends of Christ who visit the tomb see it. We inherit it. Tonight the disciples James and John are not the only people who can claim the nickname the Bible gives them, Sons of Thunder. We, thanks to God's mighty act in raising Christ, can claim that name and title as inheritors of Christ's saving resurrection: *Children of Thunder.*

The
Last Word

As I look at you and at what has just taken place when our beloved organgrinder made the thunder and the choristers reached down for their hidden handbells to create the racket we call the "Holy Noise," I wonder how true the description is of us Episcopalians as "God's Frozen People"? That sound is symbolic. It is symbolic of God *having the last word.*

Death's victory has lasted three days. And in the darkness of death and the silence of the tomb, God has caused an explosion of power. He has blown the stone away for the light of dawn to come into it, and for the life of resurrection to walk out of it. The writer of the letter to the Ephesians, in talking about the vast resources of God's power open to those who trust in him, mentions that these resources "are measured by his strength and the might which he exerted in Christ when he raised him from the dead" (Ephesians 1:19-20).

What he is saying is that this mighty act of God, in raising Jesus, is the yardstick of all his accomplishments in creation. Everything he does must be seen against that extraordinary explosion of love that blew the stone away and brought Christ to his feet to move among his friends with the news that, as the hymn says,

> Death's mightiest powers have done their worst,
> And Jesus hath his foes dispersed.

The initiative lies with God the Father. When things are dark, God acts. When life is dead, when human possibilities are finished and powers are exhausted, God acts. When hope is killed, God acts. When upon the failure of human achievement a crushing weight of stone now rests, sealed and secure for the rest of human time, God acts. That stone, that imprisoning stone, is moved, and resurrection light floods the darkness of the tomb, and from the tomb, into the world. The world is made new because of it. Beyond hope, beyond calculation, beyond the wildest reach of our imagination, there is the power of God. And that power is exercised most mightily upon Christ, for God breaks the bars of iron asunder which death has forged, so that death yields the victory to God. But that is not the end of the matter.

The end concerns us: our job is to know the power of Christ's resurrection. This, for Saint Paul, is one of the supreme aims of his life:

> All I care for is to know Christ, to *experience the power of his resurrection*...if only I may finally arrive at the resurrection from the dead. (Philippians 3:10-11)

It can happen in your life. God can *make* it happen in your life. Your life. Because the Risen Christ wants to come and share it. And if he does, and if you allow him in, if you want him to live in you, he will—as Saint Paul could shout: "Nevertheless, I live: yet not I, but Christ it is who lives in me!"

EASTERTIDE

These five sermons for Eastertide begin on the feast of the Resurrection—Easter Sunday—and move through the gospel stories of the appearances of the Risen Lord to his disciples until his ascension to heaven.

The first, "Faith at Risk," is the conclusion of the Lenten sermon course entitled "Seven Denials: The Best at Risk."

Faith
at Risk

This is the Day of Days, the Crown of the Year, the day of release and victory for the truth of God's unstoppable love declaring itself in a mighty initiative taken by him: God has blown away the stone from the mouth of the tomb and raised Christ to resurrection life. There has been a Big Bang, the explosion of God's power with Christ. This is why we can rejoice with Paul when he proclaims,

> For now is Christ risen from the dead, and become the firstfruits of them that slept. (1 Corinthians 15:20)

Wherever you look, on whatever news channel you choose, in whatever newspaper you pick, you see and hear people making flat denials. Ordinary citizens, policemen, lawyers: all make denials about what they saw or heard or said. Politicians have been in the habit of making denials to their constituents and to each other. Truth and integrity, humility, credibility, and justice are at risk in their denials. These very qualities at risk as a result of a denial are what specifically we have considered in the Sunday Lenten sermon course here at Saint Thomas this year.

It should come as no surprise to us so far away in time from the event that there is an occasion of denial on the part of somebody very close to Christ after his resurrection. Mark says that there was *disbelief* on the part of Christ's disciples when Mary Magdalene ran to tell them that she had seen and spoken to him. But disbelief and denial are not necessarily the same thing. Disbelief is a reaction. Denial can be a pro-active move. It falls to our old friend and patron, Saint Thomas, to make a flat denial.

Christ suddenly appears to the rest of the disciples as they huddle for safety behind locked doors on the Sunday evening. They are terrified of discovery and arraignment by the Jewish authorities, we are told. It is late at night. The problem of Jesus will not go away, and they fear for their own skins. Thomas, "the Twin," is not among them. He has taken himself off to suffer his heartbreak alone.

We know of his attachment to Christ. He has boasted that he would follow Christ and die with Christ. But here is someone who also expects the worst, and when the worst happens he is shattered. We often say that misery loves company. That is true for many if not most. But it doesn't include Thomas. Like an injured animal, he will take himself away from human company to lick his wounds in private and stay there until he recovers sufficiently or dies.

The sudden appearance of Christ among the frightened group, his recognition by them, his crucifixion wounds bared to them as proof, his repeated greeting of "Peace be with you," his charge to them, his conferring of the Holy Spirit by his breathing over them—all these meet a stolid and determined wall with Thomas. The excited people break their noses on the door of his denial.

"Unless I see the mark of the nails on his hands, unless I put my finger into the place where the nails were, and my hand into his side, I will not believe it." (John 20:25)

Thomas will not move an inch until he has not only seen but handled the evidence. He is not prepared for hearsay. Personal testimony from not one but ten disciples and the women meet with a wall of stubborn denial. He is in effect saying, "No way. No way. This cannot have happened. You have dreamt this up. This is wish fulfillment on your part. You want to believe he joined you at a time when you were terrified out of your wits. When you're dead, you're dead!"

People are capable of believing what they want to believe. We have only to look at the David Koresh community to realize that the members wanted to believe claims he had made in the face of history and logic and even common sense. When people do this we describe their condition as being "brainwashed." In the seventies and eighties, hoards of youngsters were persuaded by a Korean preacher to leave families and friends for a relationship based upon extraordinary claims and wild assertions. These Moonies, as they were called, wanted to believe him.

In Christ's day Zealots gathered into walled communities to safeguard their ethnic purity and to await their vindication. Harsh demands, stern rules, and inflated expectations brought in those whose imaginations were stirred and passions aroused. They wanted to believe that this was the way, and there was no other.

Thomas is somebody for whom anything out of the ordinary is not necessarily to be enthused over. You can't picture him leading you into a nouvelle cuisine restaurant. He would not be the most adventurous of your friends. And he is the epitome of the character who, when an experiment has been tried and has failed, discourages people from trying it again. We all know them. We have one in every family, usually. You can't picture him leading the shuttle team at NASA.

The trouble with our patron saint and Christ's stalwart and courageous supporter is that Thomas is deficient in religious imagination. His denial displays that deficiency. And that deficiency jeopardizes faith; it puts faith at risk. You can surround him by friends to whom something extraordinary has happened. You can barely hear him for all the shouting and the excitement, with everybody talking at once. Their literally earth-shaking experiences of Christ's appearance among them at the very time when they have not been at their best—stunned by the betrayal and arrest, wiped away by his execution and the final humiliations that preceded it, scared out of their minds by the knowledge that the vengeful authorities are after them—make no difference to Thomas. The fact that in the middle of their corporate misery and defeat the Lord had joined them and had taken charge of the group, pulling it together and giving it a new direction, a new purpose, a new vocation, a new life to experience, makes no impression on Thomas' imagination. None at all.

His faith has been reduced to the *quantitative*. He will not believe unless he can see and touch and measure with his eye the wound damage: explore the wounds themselves, and assess from the totality of his calculations the truth that his emotional friends are falling over themselves in their frenzy to declare to him. Faith cannot flourish in this straitjacket. Tie faith down to evidence that is quantifiable, that you can weigh and measure, and when you are done, it's not faith you have, but evidence.

How do you *know* when you embark upon marriage that you will be loving the person you give yourself to for life—which is the Christian church's expectation of your commitment—even more strongly after the vicissitudes of the marriage experience? You don't know. You can't know. But you go ahead and marry anyhow. It's partly instinct, with a lot of hope, and the faith that impels you to embrace the new life "in scorn of consequences."

How can you be *certain* that spring will give way to summer heat, and summer to harvesting time? You don't know. But you go ahead and plant your corn anyway. It's partly instinct, with a lot of hope and faith that the Creator of all life will cause the seed of corn to sprout, and the sprout to grow and bear fruit. You act in faith as though the truth of your purpose will declare itself. This is what the Bible means by those who "walk by faith, not by sight" (2 Corinthians 5:7).

Thomas refuses to walk by faith and not by sight; he denies belief unless he sees and touches and handles the body of the resurrected Christ. Have you wondered what his friends think at this denial? We know what happens. Christ appears a week later in that same room, locked for safety as usual. Christ is suddenly there with them, and this time Thomas is there to hear Christ's greeting and to see him. Not only that. To be invited to handle the physical evidence of the wounds of crucifixion. And to hear Christ declare, "Happy are they who never saw me and yet have found faith."

That is us. That is his promise to us, for us. That we shall be given joy. His joy. New life in the face of all evidence to the contrary is what Christians affirm this Easter morning. Ridiculous. Unbelievable. Irrational. But true. Why true?

If we don't see him, we see him in others mysteriously and powerfully living this resurrection life in them, changing them subtly, but changing them profoundly. Paul told the new Christians in Rome:

> Adapt yourselves no longer to the pattern of this present world, but *let your minds be remade* and your whole nature thus transformed. (Romans 12:2)

Paul is saying something about attitude—that overworked and tired word. Christ's resurrection life can transform your attitude. You see things differently. You react differently. Your initiatives start from a different place. Less defensive, less self-concerned, less status-conscious, less title-conscious, less socially-conscious, less money-conscious. Dying to self, in fact. You see that happening in people when Christ gets under their skin after they have invited him to come in and bring his resurrection life with him.

They begin to live. They begin to *think,* as well as *hope.* Relationships are viewed differently. Compassion grows. Patience grows. Death is seen differently, just as fears and frustrations assume different complexions. Faith flourishes because it is free from the fetters of the quantitative, the grudging evidence-weighing. People begin to savor what the Bible calls "the liberty of the children of God." And then *you* can say, like Paul, "Nevertheless I live. Yet not I, but it is Christ who lives in me!"

Christ and the
Good Old Days

I f you have the stomach for it, see the movie *Schindler's List*. You will know that it is the story of an unattractive, hard-drinking womanizer with an idea for making a fortune from armaments in the war which Nazi Germany created. Schindler is a paid-up, badge-carrying, swastika-sporting member of the Nazi party from Czechoslovakia with a factory hiring forced Jewish labor. The story of this man's involvement with the lives of hundreds of Jews from the Warsaw Ghetto in Poland whom he ransoms with the millions he has made will etch a memory on your souls with acid. The mindless, revolting sadism of the German occupation forces will unnerve you as it unnerved me.

And then remember the ultra-rightist neo-Nazi demonstrations that loomed over the international soccer game that was to be played recently on Hitler's birthday (of all days) in the very same, now infamous stadium where the 1936 Nazi-dominated Olympics rejected a black contestant and where the English soccer team was required to deliver a Nazi salute, *heil Hitler*, and were photographed doing so. That the match was canceled helps little. The

point is that there are still human souls besotted with nostalgia for the good old days of brutality and racial hatred.

The politics of nostalgia. You heard today Luke's account of the defeated and dispirited little group meeting
in the Upper Room, scared, bereft of the man who had
made their little world seem so big, who had opened the
eyes of their imaginations, broadened their horizons,
raised their hopes, made the future exciting, and who had
set the establishment on its ear with the challenges and
the criticisms and the comparisons he had made. All
gone. Gone was the energy for anything except self-preservation and nostalgia. You heard these words,

> As they were talking about all this, there he was, standing
> among them. Startled and terrified, they thought they
> were seeing a ghost. But he said, "Why are you so per-
> turbed? Why do questionings arise in your minds?"
> (Luke 24:36-38)

Startled and terrified, the disciples are rooted to the
spot of their despair. The good old days, the exciting old
days, the days of shared hopes, were over. Why turn the
knife in the wound of their grief? Even after hearing him
tell them to touch and see his hands and his feet, "they
were still unconvinced, still wondering, for it seemed too
good to be true."

While I was thinking about this and what it could
mean for us, bells began ringing in my memory. I had
read part of one of John Donne's sermons once that he
had preached upon the death of King James I, on April
26, 1625. I searched for it yesterday and found it. There is
a curious Upper Room-despair-and-bereavement air to it
that you can catch, despite its faded language and vocabu-
lary:

When you shall find that hand that had signed to one of
you a Patent for Title, to another for Pension, to another
for Pardon, to another for Dispensation, *Dead*:

That hand that settled Possessions by his Seale, in the
Keeper...and distributed to the Poore, in his Almoner, and
Health to the Diseased, by his immediate Touch, *Dead:*

That hand that ballanced his own three Kingdomes so
equally...and carried the Keyes of all the Christian world,
and locked up, and let out Armies in their due season,
Dead:...

When you see that Hand, which was the hand of
Destinie, of Christian Destinie, of the Almighty God, lie
dead....It was not so *hard* a hand when we touched it last,
nor so *cold* a hand when we kissed it last.[1]

Nobody, it seems, could be deader than a dead king.

Don't you discern some similarity in the disciples'
desolation? Everything was over. It was gone. Their faith
had died with the man they had trusted, and deserted.
They were unwilling to realize that the situation could be
subtly but entirely different from how they viewed it.
They were imprisoned in nostalgic bereavement—in
which also there was guilt, remember, in their case.

I often wonder about people who have an obsessive nostalgia. They long for the good old days they themselves
often never saw or experienced at all, or only shared to
some minor extent, and from an inferior angle. You have
only to read the novel from which that beautiful movie
was made, *The Remains of the Day,* to see how the old butler's view about life in his dead father's days as butler was

---

1   Pearsall Smith, *Donne's Sermons: Selected Passages* (Oxford: 1950).

totally and entirely of his own making. He was indulging in the politics of nostalgia when he refused to face contemporary truths about the days before the Second World War, where he experienced from behind the green baize door of some large country house the attitudes of his employer's friends and colleagues who were set to appease the greed and grandiosity of the Nazi regime.

In a harmless way—though it can be just as irritating—there are Christians who fondly look back on their church in earlier decades of its history as being the golden age. They sigh for old days and old customs which may never have resembled their picture of them. Not that this is a twentieth-century phenomenon. Back in the fourth century some Christians were moaning that once they had chalices of wood and bishops made of gold; now their chalices were golden and they were saddled with wooden bishops. Nostalgia can distort.

Back to the bedraggled bunch of miserable disciples, huddled together for mutual comfort in their nostalgic bereavement and guilt, unnerved by the sudden realization that they have been joined by Somebody Else. See what Christ does.

Christ is at pains to make his resurrection-reality recognized by the people who have been with him. He shows them his hands and his feet. He invites them to touch and examine. He goes out of his way, so to speak, to add another proof of his reality. He eats their food, their fish, with them. He talks in a way they recognize as authentically his. What other proof can you reasonably ask for? See somebody, hear somebody, watch somebody do what you're in the middle of doing?

What is the gospel saying? Isn't it saying: This is what the Lord requires of you to take seriously? To distrust nostalgia? To pull yourselves together to face *his* reality?

Isn't it saying: This is the way for the Christian community to go; to be glad in the conviction that Jesus lives, and lives in a way you can not only be glad about, but also talk about, from the shared experience of the apostles to whom Christ emphasized and underlined his resurrection-reality?

Isn't it also saying: Left to ourselves, we are incapable of recognizing resurrection-reality until—as to the men on the Emmaus Road when Christ *opened their eyes* and to the frightened little group in Jerusalem trapped by their fears and guilt when Christ *opened their minds*—we are helped by him to face this reality?

Obviously we are incapable by ourselves of recognizing resurrection. Christ has to help us. People perhaps look for the wrong things when they hope to recognize Jesus. He is unrecognizable to people who indulge in nostalgia. He is unrecognizable to them in their preoccupation with priorities that aren't necessarily his.

Only when the heart is at its most vulnerable does he make himself known, make himself understood to people in his resurrected life. *And we can only know him in his resurrected life.* Perhaps he's with you, and you haven't recognized him. Yet. Because your heart isn't ready. This possibility exists for you. You may want to pursue it....

Perceptions

The events of this week in Los Angeles have disturbed us, frightened a lot of people, made people despair. The terror and lawlessness and outburst of angry frustration; the number of violent deaths and the wanton destruction—these events have been a nightmare. It has been a week of *perceptions*. The general perception seems to be that the process of law is flawed and faulty; that somehow the cogs of justice fail to mesh, and things have gone haywire in the legal system, and that this verdict, is, shall we say, questionable?

Then among a large segment of the community is the perception that justice has been denied *them*; that if you're black you cannot *expect* justice; that if you're black you are likely to be denied the justice that would be given to other ethnic groups. Neither you nor I have sat in that suburban court; neither you nor I have listened to the arguments of the prosecution and the defense; neither you nor I have been in the jury room trying to reach a conclusion on the basis of what was heard. But all of us have seen not once but many times the scenes from the video taken of a man being beaten with police sticks; and who is to ridicule the old saying that an outsider may see most of the game?

There is a third perception. I leave it to you to judge in your heart of hearts and before God if it is fair and right.

The perception is of what is called *the thin blue line*. It is the protective layer of police defense in crime, that they must do what they must do in order to combat it, and we just don't want to know what they do to maintain order. That is the third perception and it is shared by many, perhaps even those nearer to the scene of what took place than we happen to be, sitting here in varying degrees of comfort in Saint Thomas.

I heard a piece of lying wisdom once, which was passed on to me by a parishioner who was puzzled and offended at it: that *perception is reality*. Perception is *not* reality. Perception can be affected by all sorts of factors. Fog can cloud it; darkness can reduce it; distance can diminish it; prejudice can hide it; anger can distort it; greed can enlarge it; failure to understand can deform it. Perception is not reality. Political systems, if you think for a moment, are based on perception. And we have been bombarded with political perceptions of one sort or another for months now. Moreover, we have witnessed the breathtaking realignment of perceptions in what was once the communist world to the east of us. People have realized that perception is not reality. Apply this to what has been happening around us this past week.

Now bring all that to the passage we heard read today in John's gospel. We heard the story of an aborted fishing expedition on the part of men whose livelihood it is. Peter and Thomas the Twin and Nathaniel and the sons of Zebedee and John and another disciple—seven of the eleven—had put out in a boat. A whole night's effort had produced nothing: hours and hours of patient looking into the water with flaming torches and throwing the nets where they perceived fish might be were wasted. Then listen to this:

Jesus said to them, "Children, have you any fish?" They answered him, "No." He said to them, "Cast the net on the right side of the boat, and you will find some." So they cast it, and now they were not able to haul it in, for the quantity of fish. That disciple whom Jesus loved said to Peter, "It is the Lord!" When Simon Peter heard that it was the Lord, he put on his clothes, for he was stripped for work, and sprang into the sea. But the other disciples came in the boat, dragging the net full of fish, for they were not far from the land, but about a hundred yards off.

When they got out on land, they saw a charcoal fire there, with fish lying on it, and bread. Jesus said to them, "Bring some of the fish that you have just caught." So Simon Peter went aboard and hauled the net ashore, full of large fish, a hundred and fifty-three of them; and although there were so many, the net was not torn.

Jesus said to them, "Come and have breakfast." Now none of the disciples dared ask him, "Who are you?" They knew it was the Lord. Jesus came and took the bread and gave it to them, and so with the fish. This was now the third time that Jesus was revealed to the disciples after he was raised from the dead. (John 21:5-14)

The resurrected Lord stands unperceived as to who he is in the grey of the early dawn. He is perceived as just an onlooker to the men, who are disgruntled and sullen in their frustration. They are near the shore, within easy shouting distance, and he asks an innocent question, knowing what the answer is: "Have you caught anything?" Of course they haven't and their answer is not likely to be a polite negative; possibly a four-letter word from a bunch of angry and disappointed partners shouted back to the man near enough to be recognizable, and yet

not recognized, not perceived as the risen Christ. You
would think they could tell him by his voice as well as by
his shape and features even before the sun comes up. It
could be that their preoccupation with their failure prevents recognition. What I suspect from what I read in the
gospel accounts is that Jesus *is* very different from what
they expect: totally unlike what they are used to.

The friendly man offers some practical advice: cast *this*
side. From where he stands he sees fish they can't see.
They land an enormous catch. And triumph is followed
by hunger as they smell breakfast cooking. Their friendly
advisor and helper who has overturned their failure is
now a kind and considerate host; and then perceptions
dawn. First the disciple whom Jesus loves, John, then Peter, recognize Christ to be the onlooker on the shore:
their risen Lord.

Don't you think it is strange that the identity of the
resurrected Christ seems always open to mistake? How
the perceptions of familiarity and past experience are always faulty when it comes to recognizing him in his resurrection life? If you read the accounts carefully you will
see that in every case recorded his self-revelation is a surprise. Nobody catches him out and about, nobody spots
him, like you do a rare bird or a wanted criminal, when he
is not expecting to be seen. It is always the fact that perceptions are mistaken.

He is perceived as a gardener by the grief-blinded Mary
Magdalene, until something in his voice triggers the recognition of his resurrection reality. He is perceived as a
lone traveler on the road to Emmaus on Easter night by
two guilty and depressed followers of his ministry—guilty
because a couple of nights ago they had deserted him, and
depressed because they had invested everything in him:

their love, their loyalty, their pride, their hopes. His extravagant claims, his extraordinary promises, his outrageous proclamations, his unsettling reminders, his impossible requirements, his unheard-of reclamations from sicknesses and sins and the death of Lazarus: he had made all these in their company. He had been the wonder of the world. Now he is dead; and when you're dead, you're dead! Something had died in them, too. Not merely their invested love and loyalty and pride and hopes. Not merely the life of the community he had imparted by his personality. Belief had been shattered. Motivation had withered. They are finished and they mourn together along the road when they are joined by a stranger who asks them why they are so depressed. That same evening Christ, at supper, makes himself known to them in the breaking of the bread.

Perceptions.

Now, my question is: is the risen Christ a reality in your life? You will remember that he cannot be spotted like a rare bird on a twig or discovered like a fugitive in disguise and surprised with his real identity. This is why I am skeptical that his reality has made itself known to a politician who sees Jesus merely as a revolutionary; or to the rich moneymakers of old as the captain of capitalistic aspirations; or to the bitter fundamentalist preaching a cruel and limited gospel; or to a sentimentalist who seeks a mushy, woolly companion. Those perceptions are not reality.

He is different from what you expect. He is different from what you may perceive. He meets you unexpectedly—always when you are not at your best; always when you are vulnerable, or very much alone in your life, and guilty, and caught out. He hides under the most improbable circumstances and persons and events. When the prospects are bleak and when old friends fail you. In a person you may disapprove of or not wish to be seen with. Disappointment may bring you to recognize him. And sickness or suffering certainly have, in the lives of people I know, as well as, if I may say so, in my own life. I know he has been there in personal triumphs and in deep happiness and high joys, but he has been hard for me to recognize in them. I have caught a glimpse of him when I have been forgiven, when I have been allowed to recover my health, when I have been given another chance in a relationship I have damaged.

I wonder, I just wonder, if he may not have quietly made himself recognizable to Rodney King, who in the middle of the Los Angeles horror could say:

> People, I just want to say, you know, can we all get along? Can we get along? Can we stop making it horrible for the older people and the kids?
>
> And I mean, we've got enough smog here in Los Angeles, let alone to deal with setting these fires and things. It's just not right. It's not going to change anything. And I'm neutral, I love everybody, I love people of color. I'm not like they're picking me out to be.
>
> We've got to quit. We've got to quit. I can understand the first upset for the two hours after the verdict, but to go on like this, to see the security guard shot on the ground, it's not right. It's just not right. Because those people can never go home to their families again.
>
> Please, we can get along here. We all can get along. I mean, we're all stuck here for a while. Let's try to work it out. Let's try to beat it. Let's try and work it out.

Was Christ there? For him?

The Dust-Bowl
of Trust

One of the saddest things I read this past week about the death of President Richard Nixon—and I have kept thinking miserably about it—was Mr. Kissinger's remark that "if only there had been somebody who loved him." But there wasn't. Apart from his wife and daughters, nobody among his colleagues, even the closest, deeply loved him. He was very much the poorer for that. He had all he wanted, but not, and never, that.

There is a terrible saying in the Psalms: "The Lord gave them their heart's desire...and sent leanness into their souls." If anything was a tragedy for Richard Nixon, it was that. There was a leanness in his soul that repelled some people, especially those who knew him well.

And it meant he had nobody to trust. Are you like that? Are you in the position of having nobody to trust? You may have people who love you and whom you love in return, but do you feel you can't trust them? Financially, morally, personally, not to speak of professionally?

It is a difficult and dangerous predicament, to have nobody to trust. When you get into this predicament you impute motive. It is usually judgmental:

Why was she so kind to me? What does she want out
of me?

Why is he so intent on friendship with me? To possess me?

Why is she so ready to lend me what I need? Does
she intend to take my enterprise out of my hands?

Why is he supporting me politically and personally?
Does he look on himself as my successor?

Why can't I find this place? Did they deliberately
give me wrong directions? Perhaps they couldn't be
bothered to give me the right ones.

Why does this priest act in this way? Isn't he a
hypocrite?

Obviously, you can make yourself not only thoroughly
miserable but also thoroughly lonely, not to mention bitter and judgmental. And people weren't created to be
lonely. God made families. Death may deplete families
and deprive individual members of the kind of companionship and support which families can give. But people
have been sustained and steadied by the help of someone
else *just being there* and reachable.

I wouldn't go so far as to support the theologically
questionable statement I saw in a health food shop on
Madison Avenue near the church: "God can't do everything, so she made mothers." All wrong! God creates not
out of a sense of need but because his love overflows and
creation ensues. The point is: we need to be *earthed*, if I
may put it like that, in relationships from which we find
ourselves able to give as much as we receive from them.
Trust flourishes in that rich earth.

If you were following the psalm so beautifully sung by
our choir today, the last verse will tell you something
wonderful about God, "who holds our souls in life, and

will not allow our feet to slip" (Psalm 66:8). It is an acute perception of God's activity among us, and what our response should be: gratitude and trust.

He holds our souls in life. I was talking to two beloved friends who are my house guests about my encounter in August 1988 with a man who attacked me from behind and smashed in my skull with a piece of lead pipe, while on my way home from supper with a parishioner.

On that first day after the previous night's activity I was lying in my bed on the seventeenth floor of the New York hospital, fully aware of what was going on around me, looking at the time, and seeing it was about four-thirty. I felt totally comfortable, surprisingly cool, and physically light. There was no trace of heaviness in my limbs or body. There wasn't an ounce of pain. There was just thankfulness and contentment to be ministered to so lovingly and competently by nurses and surgeons and people like our vicar. I remember the happiness of it, quiet and complete.

That was the hour when the doctors feared I was dying. I felt supported by love: the everlasting arms of God bearing me up palpably and very obviously to me. I found it easier to talk to God than usual. In happy trust in our Lord I asked him to forgive my attacker, because I could never believe he knew what he was doing. I felt very close to the prayers of my parish family for me, their strength and their urgency—*and the faith* that was in those prayers supporting my recovery. I began to recover from that moment, so rapidly that I overheard two young surgeons say something to the effect that "Father John's recovery was *miraculous*," a week or so later. It was obvious they had trust, trust that was vouchsafed and given to me in that wonderful hour of happiness and support.

God gives you trust. But you must take it. The bad worker always blames his own tools. God puts a mighty weapon in your hands if you will reach out for him to give it to you. I know this to be true. How do I know? I look at Christ; what he does in the garden of Gethsemane as he pours out his heart, with his sweat like tears of blood, to the Father, whose will is Christ's obedient will.

"Take the chalice from me," Jesus says. Then, "No. Thy will be done." He holds us up: us and the whole creation— "He's got the whole world in his hands." He not only holds our souls in life; he will not allow our feet to slip.

His hands support us. They also take ours if we will reach out to his, to lead us. This is no pollyanna, pious talk. It is the conviction and the testament of many people to whom God has made a difference in their lives. A taxi driver who told me his name was Tony Rampoulla said this to me at the red light on 53rd Street and Fifth Avenue as I was getting out: "I found two or three years ago that God makes all the difference. Life is completely changed for me." And he said it not in that nauseous, self-conscious, "I'm saved" way, but determinedly and quietly and shyly. Tony trusts in God not merely to keep him, but to keep him going. Doesn't Christ underline all this when he says, "I am with you *always,* to the end of time"?

Back, then, to this self-killing attitude of refusal to trust other people, of imputing the motives of others, of scowling, as it were, at an opportunity to enlarge your life by enlarging your friendships, to be happy to look for the goodness in others, to cease to fear their less good, subhuman sides, and from that fear to make decisions that may be smart but cruel, prudent but unjust, based on racial prejudice, social prejudice, sexual prejudice, and hatreds of all kinds of people.

It is not the same as having one's confidence in somebody else shattered. It is not the same as "once bitten,
twice shy." It is not the same as wariness after betrayal, or
caution after deception, or being unnerved after a fearful
disappointment or hurt. *All these are reactions.* To be suspicious because you do not have previous experience of a
person even where there is little need to be suspicious, to
despise on sight an appearance or an accent: this is refusing to believe that "God holds our souls in life, and will
not allow our feet to slip."

Our Lord makes sure his disciples understand the prin-
ciples of this:

> "Trust in God always; trust also in me. There are many
> dwelling-places in my Father's house; if it were not so I
> should have told you; for I am going there on purpose to
> prepare a place for you. And if I go and prepare a place for
> you, I shall come again and receive you to myself, so that
> where I am you may be also." (John 14:1-3)

If ever there was a reassurance as we approach the feast
of the Ascension, this is it. Practice your trust by examining yourself for unworthy suspicions, useless suspicions,
suspicions cherished and hoarded like money hidden, for
"where your treasure is, there will your heart be also,"
and exorcise them, for Christ's sake.

The
Mustard Seed

As sportsman Yogi Berra said, "It's *déja vu* all over again." I look at the Scriptures set for this day and I recall some years ago commenting on the number of the faithful facing Peter after the eleven had returned from taking leave of the Lord on Mount Olivet. As the author of the Acts of the Apostles described them, the total body of believers—disciples included—would have filled the first half of our small Chantry Chapel. About one hundred and twenty in all. And that was all. One hundred twenty. The lot. That is all there was.

That little group in Jerusalem: not many, and not very impressive—it's not as though the one hundred twenty were from the first four hundred families of snobbish New York. What is the proportion to the population? We are told that in Palestine in those days there were about four million inhabitants, so the ratio is fewer than one in thirty thousand. Apply that to New York: for eight million you could calculate two hundred forty Christians.

One hundred twenty people. Now you see what the task is? To persuade others from that four million, to convince others of the truth of Jesus being alive and among them after he had suffered the death experience, is a daunting task. Where do you start? From within your one hundred twenty there are eleven disciples who have been around Jesus from his baptism by John in the Jordan until he left them for heaven. Think of it. Think if *this* congregation were the size to fit comfortably and with one or two empty pews in the Chantry Chapel. Everybody would know everybody. That's a plus, perhaps. But there would be no place for the old-fashioned Episcopalians described as "God's frozen chosen." There would be no solitary Christians leading a private Christian life.

I am trying to help you place the other end of the telescope to your eye, to help you imagine what the job is like for a group of people that size. But that little group manages to "turn the whole world upside down" (Acts 17:6). That is what the gospel does. It turns everything on its head. It makes big things seem little in importance. It makes insignificant things world-size.

Think how Christ in his ministry keeps banging this particular drum. He talks of a mustard seed, the tiniest speck of a seed, growing into a bird-sheltering bush. He talks of a kernel of wheat falling to the ground to die in order to produce over a hundred times its number. He talks about a tiny coin tossed into the Temple offertory box by the little old lady on starvation-level being worth infinitely more than the riches of the rich. He talks about a cup of cold water bringing life to someone in terrible need. He talks about sparrows being watched by their heavenly Creator.

He takes the tiny, forgettable things that were too familiar for us to notice or give credit for, and holds them up for us to realize and assess their breathtaking value. He talks about the least of these his little ones, and their eternal worth. There is nothing of no value. There is no tiny child who cannot teach us something about being included in the kingdom of heaven. All these teaching pictures of Christ are with his own resurrection in mind—the upside-downness of things in the divine plan for us. Small beginnings, small re-beginnings.

You and I are witnessing a phenomenon, if we have eyes to see. The church in Russia was almost extinguished by the direct policy of the Marxist Communists in power. Churches were looted, systematically, the buildings either destroyed out of hand or put to secular use as prisons or warehouses or museums. Much treasure was looted and sold; its bishops and priests and monks and nuns were massacred in their thousands or went to unknown graves in the prisons and mines of Siberia. Church teaching was forbidden; church schools were closed, seminaries were shut down, monasteries destroyed and the communities disposed.

It was a systematic strangulation of the religious life until the rivers of the spirit became a rare trickle, and the dark night of the soul covered a land which formerly was lit with a myriad of lamps of devotion. The clergy who were left somehow had to make an accommodation with the state in order to reach anybody. It is easy for us in the comfort of our armchairs to make judgments about the methods they used to keep alive. It is very easy to stand on high moral ground in a country where freedom of expression has been exploited, and criticize what people have been obliged to settle for: for the sake of their families and their children, not to mention their own lives.

And now the night is over. The church of Russia is "gathering up the fragments that remain, that nothing be lost." Those fragments are not only scattered, and tiny.

They are damaged by the savage trampling of godless boots for seventy years.

The work is delicate, tentative, and protracted, but the determination is there to obey our Lord's command to his disciples to find and gather the crumbs, the particles, that nothing be lost. Slowly churches in Russia are being rehabilitated by the faithful with whatever they can raise among themselves to put the damage right. Slowly monasteries and seminaries are starting up again, without the things they so sorely need, like books and Scriptures. They are adept at making do. Hospitals under the aegis of the church—one of its glories—are being taken back and equipment is painfully being brought up-to-date. There is a lack of everything material and financial. But there is no lack of fire: the determination to bring Christ back to Russia, to restore the ravages of the years, the "years that the locust hath eaten."

A remarkable priest heads the resurrection-life of the church in Russia, the Patriarch Alexei II. He is a person young enough to have reserves of powerful energy of mind and spirit and devotion and ingenuity to inspire the work of rehabilitation and expansion of his damaged church. The determination is contagious, and with new life there are new needs.

A link has been established between our diocese of New York and the Moscow Patriarchate, and some form of partnership is beginning. Bishop Richard Grein and some priests and people, including myself, are going to Moscow on a diocesan pilgrimage this summer for ten days. On the pilgrimage we shall see something of what the church in the Moscow area is attempting to do to recover and re-establish the spiritual life of the thousands who long to be ministered to and to let the light of the Spirit into their

lives. It's *déja vu* all over again, really. We are witnesses to
a rebirth of the church, and we have within our sights a
powerful lesson we would do well to learn and make our
own.

The secret is the refusal to be intimidated and the determination to let people know the good news. No matter
how small. No matter how insignificant. No matter how
puny. If you know Christ you have the challenge which
Peter, straight from his experience of witnessing the dis-
appearance of Jesus from earthly sight, gives to you. It
won't take the form of nagging someone into saying Yes, I
believes Christ Jesus to be alive. "A man convinced
against his will, will hold the same opinions still." That
little chantry-chapel of people didn't *nag* so much as *win,*
because people could see in them the evidence of the
truth they were claiming: that Jesus lives! Fifty days after
the feast of Passover, on the day of Pentecost, the whole
lot were powerfully visited by Christ in the Holy Spirit,
who rained tongues of fire in a whirlwind of divine activity, and they emerged the living embodiment of the unstoppable power of the insignificant.

It is this which keeps me going. When I know that *in
spite of me* the things I know to be true and eternal can
gain a foothold in another person's life; that somewhere
along the path of my life's pilgrimage, my faith, despite
the caricature my personality makes of it, *can* somehow
strike a spark in the tinder of someone's dry soul, then I
am strengthened to go on. When a friend with AIDS and
fearful at the prospect of the lonely journey soon to be
taken can find some comfort and reassurance in things
said from the pulpit or in private conversation, then I am
strengthened to go on. When someone damaged by physical violence or brutal neglect in a friendship or betrayal in

a marriage can seek and discover peace and healing in the worship here, then I am strengthened to go on.

Wherever God places us, whatever he allows us to be and allows us to do in that place and with the souls around us, there are opportunities given for the life of the risen Christ to display itself in us. For nothing is of no importance to him who loves us and gave himself for us.

PENTECOST

It is usually a mistake to ignore the Scriptures assigned by the church for that particular day when you are trying to decide what to preach about. The discipline is salutary. It prevents hobbyhorse-riding, and it requires some hours of research and reflection, biblically and theologically.

These sermons have been preached, pretty well all of them, in the summer and fall of the year, in the long green season of Pentecost or Trinitytide, as many of us know it. Thus they cover a fairly wide field, from conversion to stewardship. One of them—"Getting Hold of the Right End of the Stick"—was preached for a specific occasion at Saint Thomas, the final Sunday for our graduating choir school boys.

On the Safe Side

You have to be brave to correct somebody in public. And on a grand occasion. My first boss would qualify. The town of Redcar where I began my priesthood had little to claim for itself. It was a blue-collar town; most of the men worked in the steel mills in the next town, Middlesborough. But it had a mayor, and the mayor was always a local boy made good.

Every year the mayor made a solemn entrance into the parish church, where I was at the time a curate in my mid-twenties. He wore the mayoral robes of scarlet and fur, complete with a great gold chain and black cockaded hat. The rector ceremonially met him at the door and accompanied him and his overheated wife to the front pew, followed by the alderman and councillors in their robes of office and their black cockaded hats.

Whatever it was that irritated the rector about that particular year's mayor, whom he had known since he was a gangling lad, I shall never know. Probably the mayor had stood on his dignity and patronized the church or had boasted of something or other that he had achieved. At any rate, the mayor had a self-satisfied smile on his face as he left the church at the end of the service. It disappeared at the door when to both my agony and my ecstasy I saw the rector turn on the mayor: "Mr. Mayor," he said, "you're complacent. Remember that it was complacency which broke our Lord's heart."

We heard a similar story today in the New Testament lesson. Paul is made to ascend Mars' Hill in Athens where the famous court, the Areopagus, would sit. Its thirty members were the judges of the Supreme Court. Paul had been apprehended in the city and taken by those who had arrested him up to the court to explain himself. The ideas he had been outlining to anyone who would stop to listen to him had sounded outrageous.

"May we know what this new doctrine is that you propound?" the inquisitive Athenians ask him. "You are introducing ideas that sound strange to us, and we should like to know what they mean." And then Luke, the author of Acts, adds a snide comment: "Now the Athenians in general and the foreigners there had no time for anything but talking or hearing about the latest novelty" (Acts 17:19-21).

The judges and the people who had seized Paul could never have been expecting to hear what he now says. Paul takes the offensive. He serves an ace:

> "Men of Athens, I see that in everything that concerns religion you are habouring superstitious fears to an uncommon degree." (Acts 17:22)

How is that for starters? Then he puts the boot in.

> "For as I was going around looking at the objects of your worship, I noticed among other things an altar bearing the inscription 'To An Unknown God'. What you worship but do not know—this is what I now proclaim."

Paul then outlines his theology of God the Creator on whom our existence depends, who cannot be reduced to the human dimension of imagination but judges his creation through his Son, whom he has raised from the dead.

That is a powerful and daring claim to make on the back of his rebuke to them for their superstitious fears. He faces incredulity, ridicule, and the response popular to this very day: "We'll talk about it later." Which means that we don't want to talk about it at all.

The unknown God. What Paul is attacking is the attempt to sidestep an issue which should be confronted. Belief in God requires commitment. An unknown God may rate an acknowledgment of sorts but requests no commitment. That acknowledgment may be, as Paul says, a superstitious fear. You acknowledge what may possibly be there for fear of offending what may possibly be there. You do it to be *on the safe side*. This attitude and practice is present with us as we press our noses to the gates of the twenty-first century. People will still prefer to be on the safe side rather than commit themselves.

There is much to be said for the present practice of prenuptial agreements. "Prenups" figure large among the wealthy, the upwardly mobile, the bright young people. They do try to ensure that a just and fair division of possessions is outlined. But am I wrong in smelling a rat (even a shampooed rat) among all this legal correctitude and preoccupation with what belongs to whom? I seem to remember the old wedding vow as the ring is placed on the bride's finger: "With this ring I thee wed; with my body I thee worship, and with all my worldly goods I thee endow." That speaks of commitment to permanency in the institution of marriage. It speaks of going out on a limb for your beloved. It speaks of risks to be taken when you declare your life no longer your own but shared and mutually possessed by your spouse.

Is it not just possible that the present passion for pre-nups bespeaks a fear not merely of possibility but of *likelihood* that those solemn vows to a life-long union may fall apart, and fall away? That the institution of marriage is a sort of unknown God, in whose direction you nod, just to be on the safe side, but with whom there is room for *non*-commitment, for playing it safe?

We do it with God himself, preferring not to get too near to him, wanting not to know too much about him, for fear that he might make his demands upon our lives in *specific.*

I talked on Friday night with an intelligent and amusing architectural designer and interior decorator who spoke of his religion in the beauty he perceives in shape and texture, in sunlight and shadow, in color and motion. He could be right in his reverence for these wonders of creation, but they make no moral demands upon him, no requirement for specific worship and allegiance beyond appreciation and general gratitude for being alive and young and able to see.

He doesn't have a personal God to have to answer to, to account to, to apologize to, before whom he can protest his love and devotion and loyalty and the pledge of his heart. He can keep his heart to himself if he wishes, for the religion he enjoys allows him to be selfish, louche and lustful, hedonistic and greedy if he chooses. There is no obligation to leave a warm bed for a hard pew or to sacrifice of what he possesses to help the unattractive, ubiquitous, inadequate panhandler. He is sensitive to the things of creation and can produce beauty himself, without the sternness of moral and spiritual discipline gladly undergone for the God who "so loved the world that he gave his only begotten Son, that all who believe in him may not perish but have everlasting life."

When you play your life of religion on these lines where there is no commitment, and therefore no concomitant demands from the unseen Giver and Lover, death becomes a horror to contemplate. You must then strive to avoid by every means at hand that unavoidable experience, to pretend it doesn't happen, and to call the experience by every name other than death: "passing on," "leaving us," or whatever.

From the beginning, however, God has made it perfectly clear to his people that he has no intention of being on the safe side. He is the God who makes himself known. He identifies himself. He identifies his people.

His wish is for his people to know him, and knowing him to love him, and loving him to serve him, and serving him to share in his life of love, that his love may be in them and his life may be lived by them. He is a hidden God, to be sure. "No man hath seen God at any time." Yet he discloses himself not merely in the wonders and beauties of his created order, in shape and texture, in sunlight and shadow, in color and motion, in all the ways that my young acquaintance finds joy without wishing to know the Creator of those wonders well enough for the Creator to claim a place in his life and affections.

God hides himself in order to make himself known, because he is not content to be or to remain unknown. God is a declaratory God.

He declares himself by divesting and laying aside the glory proper to Godhead and taking up the flesh of a human and subjecting himself to the limits and the vulnerabilities of humanity, so that when we look at Christ we see God, and when we hear Christ we hear God, and when Christ puts pressure upon us it is God putting us on the narrow path his Son has had to walk, uphill to Calvary with the cross on his shoulders and through death's gates, to the light and life of resurrection beyond.

It is some time since you heard a piece of preaching from my favorite poet, John Donne, whom have I described as the scamp-turned-priest, the fornicator turned ineffable spokesman of the eternal gospel. On January 30, 1625, the Sunday after the Conversion of Saint Paul, in Saint Paul's Cathedral, John Donne said:

> Princes are God's Trumpet, and the Church is God's Organ, but Christ Jesus is his Voice. When he speaks in the Prince, when he speaks in the Church, there we are bound to hear, and happy if we do hear. Man hath a natural way to come to God, by the eye, by the creature; so visible things show the invisible God; but then, God hath superinduced a supernatural way, by the ear. For though hearing be natural, yet that faith in God should come by hearing a man preach, is supernatural.
>
> God shut up the natural way, in Paul, seeing; he struck him blind; but he opened the supernatural way, he enabled him to hear, and to hear him. God would have us beholden to grace, and not to nature, and to come for our salvation, to his Ordinances, to the preaching of his word, and not to any other means.[1]

Nearly 370 years have not faded the power of that vivid picture. I could wish I had had that book of Donne's sermons to hand when my young dinner acquaintance spoke

---

1   Pearsall Smith, *Donne's Sermons: Selected Passages* (Oxford: 1950), 141.

so enthusiastically of his unknown God, the God whose fingerprints he preferred to glimpse but whose voice he chose not to hear, for what God says would tie him down, and what Christ asks would cost too much. For Christ talks of harsh reality and stern curtailment of the undisciplined self, of sacrifice and of cross-carrying if we are to arrive at the place he has gone to prepare for us.

Far from being content to be remote and unknown by humanity, Christ seeks the companionship that commitment to him brings. He thirsts for our friendship, he calls us friends. He discloses God to us in his companionship:

> "If you knew me you would know my Father too. From now on you do know him; you have seen him." Philip said to him, "Lord, show us the Father and we ask no more." Jesus answered, "Have I been all this time with you, Philip, and you still do not know me? Anyone who has seen me has seen the Father. Then how can you say 'Show us the Father'? Do you not believe that I am in the Father, and the Father in me?" (John 14:7-10)

Wasted Lives

How often do we take individuals and institutions for granted? Occasionally they can jerk us from our complacency and we realize how valuable they are. *The New York Times* is one such in my life. The daily catalogue of calamities in the world and in New York alone can numb my sensibilities. The temptation to be irritated by ecclesiastical or ethnic eccentricities and exaggerations gives place to gratitude for some beautifully written piece about something we've never suspected or known even to exist.

One such story was on the science pages and was called, "To Drive Away Wasps, Caterpillars Recruit a Phalanx of Ants." Did you know (I didn't) that there is a mysterious rapport between certain butterfly caterpillars and some ants? The caterpillars eat leaves which produce an acid these ants like. The caterpillars enjoy their meal and send out vibrations, a sound like "running a comb over the edge of a table," which the ants pick up from the reverberations running through the plant, and come to milk the ants of the amino acid.

Enter the villain of the piece, stage right: the wasps. Wasps enjoy fat caterpillars for lunch. They try to make a pounce but the ants give them such a good bite when *their* friendly food is threatened that the wasps are discouraged and fly off. So the complexities of ecology, the kaleidoscope of mutual dependency between differing species, are maintained mysteriously in the workings of Creation. Balance is maintained. Beautiful butterflies are brought safely into the sunshine; ants are well fed with what does them good; and wasps have to work harder for their lunch. *Waste is avoided.*

I wonder if you caught a reference to waste in the lesson read from Saint John's gospel this morning? It is from the sixth chapter, and if you place the lesson in its proper place in the gospel, you will see that the miracle of the feeding of the five thousand has taken place shortly before our reading.

You will remember that after that extraordinary event, when five thousand had been fed and satisfied after an unpromising start, the disciples were required by Christ to go through the picnic area and collect the leftovers: "Gather up the fragments that remain, that nothing be lost" (John 6:12).

There is something in the divine character which deprecates waste, which will not entertain the presence of waste. Creation is no slap-happy, careless affair. It is a meticulous, painful exercise, very costly to God. How do I know? I'll tell you how I know. Christ describes his Father's activity and his own in terms of hard, sweaty, ditch-digging, road-making slog. "My Father labors," he says, "and I labor, too" (John 5:17).

Don't for a minute imagine creation to be a touch of the fairy wand stuff, putting an instant sparkle on things and making princes out of frogs. It has a component of agony, like birth-pains. Wastefulness has no place in the divine plan. Everything is too precious. And you heard Jesus say about his Father,

"I did not come from heaven to do what I want! I came to do what the Father wants me to do. He sent me, and he wants to make certain that none of the ones he has given me will be lost. Instead he wants me to raise them to life on the last day." (John 6:38-39)

God has a preoccupation with oversight and guardianship. The divine love which brought us into the world with birth-pains shared by him with our mothers counts us infinitely and eternally precious. Christ hits that same nail on the head when he teaches about sparrows, not one of which, he says, can fall to the ground unnoticed by its Creator. And are we not worth far more than a precious sparrow? The love that makes the world go 'round will not countenance waste, does not contemplate a wastage system.

It is this consideration which disturbs me so profoundly in the bitter arguments over abortion. Conscientiously and carefully the arguments for and against the rights of women to choose what happens to their bodies have to take on board the consideration of the wish and will of our Creator in his detestation of waste. All human rights arguments, with which we have a duty to come to honest terms, are based upon divine foundations: that we are made in the image of God, and bear his spark and share his life. True. That same loving Father expressly deprecates waste and we are required to be aware of that in all our considerations of human rights. It is my duty to lay that premise before you. It is your duty to apply that premise to any consideration you choose to make in matters as fraught and as sensitive as this. We have to think our faith through.

But what do you say to the waste of a life you have watched develop and blossom? We are free as humans to make up our own minds, for the most part. True it is that all of us carry around a suitcase-load of inhibitions and individual impediments of one sort or another, absorbed long ago and taken on without our noticing them much. To some extent we are all impeded. What do you say of those who appear hell-bent on squandering all their lives and bruising the lives of those around them? With drugs? With alcohol? With singleminded selfishness? With depravity of one sort or another? Those whom the psalmist describes as "delighting in lies"? The fundamentally dishonest? The vengeful and the vindictive?

The fact is that, in one way or another and sometimes in several ways at once, human lives *are* piddled away, wasted, squandered, never brought to the fulfillment for which they were made despite the gifts—or the lack of them—with which they were endowed. And what do you say about the self-destructiveness that wrecks relationships as well as health, or even life itself? There is a sad mystery of lives poured out needlessly, both in peace and time of war, when the promise and the future hold out much joy and fulfillment.

Then again, in a church like this, many come, many go. We see them come, and my hope always is that they are made welcome by the members of the parish family, so that they want to come back because they feel they are wanted. They come back, a good number of them, and we hope to include them in the mission of the church itself, which is to carry the good news out with them and light a path which others may choose to put themselves along. They can do this in all sorts of ways, by involving themselves with people who so desperately need help and cannot do much to help themselves: the hungry and the destitute, the homeless, those infected with killing diseases, those in slavery to drugs or alcohol, those whose minds no longer work for them. They can help the church here with their own expertise: with the physical fabric of this great building, with the finances for its upkeep and repair; with teaching the people new to the faith or helping with our school for the little ones who are our future. With telephoning the lonely and the sick. With the work of worship and the maintenance of our liturgies.

Others come, and for whatever reason, they do not stay. There is in every Christian community a *pastoral wastage.* This troubles me. I can understand and sympathize with those souls who find in other churches a more challenging presentation of the gospel, or in other denominations an emphasis their spirit needs. I can understand all that, and I can sympathize with it. What worries me is the disillusionment some people say they feel, and so they leave. Obviously they join us with expectations. Some weigh us in the balance and find us wanting because we fail to emphasize the things they think are most important.

How we can at one and the same time open our arms in welcome *and* fill their hunger *and* provide them with ministries to fulfill is the challenge which at times daunts me, because I am responsible before God for pastoral wastage, and I must heed the requirement of my Savior to "gather up the fragments that remain, that nothing be lost." And sadly, some are, at least to us.

The consolation I can glean is that they may find the fulfillment which their souls cry for, so that "they are saved by Christ forever," as the old Prayer Book so beautifully expresses it. For the work of reclamation and recon-

ciliation is something Christians have as a foremost task.
Saint Paul tells us so unequivocally:

> From first to last this has been the work of God. He has
> reconciled us to himself through Christ, and he has en-
> listed us in this service of reconciliation. What I mean is,
> that God was in Christ reconciling the world to him-
> self,...and that he has entrusted us with the message of
> reconciliation. We come therefore as Christ's ambassa-
> dors. It is as if God were appealing to you through us: in
> Christ's name, we implore you, be reconciled to God! (2
> Corinthians 5:18-20)

Hooked!

Some of you may remember my telling you of the Scots Presbyterian minister who could never get off the subject of infant baptism in his sermons. His elders got together with him to discuss this obsession of his and suggested that *they* should choose the biblical texts upon which he should hang his pulpit remarks. He accepted the suggestion and was given the text, "Whither Goest Thou?" When he got into the pulpit the next Sunday, he began: "My text this morning, 'Whither Goest Thou?', has three points: first, Where is it that you are coming from?; second, What it is that you hope to achieve when you get there?; and third, Infant baptism...."

It may well be that as the weeks go on I shall run the risk of obsessional tenacity to the theme of stewardship. Each individual Christian soul is given responsibility to take account of what he or she enjoys from God, to give thanks, and in gratitude to give back to God, the loving Giver and Provider, a portion for the continuance of the Creation. In this way each of us takes our rightful share in what the Scriptures call maintaining "the fabric of the world.

The lessons this morning speak of the recurring theme of God's liberality, his constant re-creating, restoring, making new, and putting right. Listen:

Blessed is he that hath the God of Jacob for his help,
  and whose hope is in the Lord his God:
Who made heaven and earth, the sea, and all that
    therein is,
    who keepeth his promise for ever;
Who helpeth them to right that suffer wrong;
    who feedeth the hungry.
The Lord looseth the prisoners:
    The Lord giveth sight to the blind.
The Lord helpeth them that are fallen;
    the Lord careth for the righteous:
The Lord careth for the strangers;
    he defendeth the fatherless and widow.
As for the way of the ungodly,
    he turneth it upside down. (Psalm 146:5-9)

And then you hear Isaiah:

Say to them that are of a fearful heart, Be strong, fear
not:...he will come and save you. Then the eyes of the
blind shall be opened, and the ears of the deaf shall be un-
stopped. Then shall the lame man leap as an hart, and the
tongue of the dumb sing: for in the wilderness shall waters break out, and streams in the desert.   (Isaiah 35:4-6)

And Christ himself:

"Ephphatha, that is, be opened." And straightway his ears
were opened, and the string of his tongue was loosed, and
he spake plain. (Mark 7:34-35)

Through psalm and prophecy and gospel narrative you
hear the chime of reclamation, of restoration, of re-crea-
tion and redemption as God works his purpose out in his
world, pouring his life into situations where there is want

and weakness and wastage. He is putting people right. He is making all things new and he "keepeth his promise for ever." That promise is something we have to come to terms with. It is the promise of *himself,* and of his self-giving. It is in this characteristic that we get a clue about God's personality. It typifies Christ. It is a *giving* characteristic. You may remember Archbishop Michael Ramsey's axiom: "God is Christlike and in him is no un-Christlikeness at all." His self-giving was total. "God so loved the world that he gave...."

Some people have a psychological need to give. Ask any fundraiser. These people need to give in order to get something else back, even if it is some form of relief from a pressure known only to them—guilt or lovelessness or loneliness or whatever. That, when you look at it, is not a good aspect of a personality motivated to give. There are compulsive givers: confronted by any request in the mail, they will respond uncritically and unsystematically and, therefore, wastefully.

And this, God is not. One of the most surprising phrases tumbles out of our Lord's mouth after the feeding of the five thousand miraculously from the lad's contribution of two loaves and a few small fishes: "Gather up the fragments that remain, that nothing may be lost." His provision may seem prodigal, to the superficial glance. The divine wastage may be astronomical, to the superficial glance. Certainly we look at the fearsome catalogue of train crashes, fire disasters, and what devastation uncontrollable weather can cause to human lives and human endeavor, or the wickedness of tyrants and cruel men the holocausts, the Armenian genocides, or the depravities of the Stalins of our day. By human mistake, by human greed, by human madness, by human ignorance, human lives are scrapped and trashed and become as though they had never been. The count is incalculable, the grief immeasurable.

But through it all it is the experience and conviction of the thinking soul that a generous and loving Creator and Redeemer walks the earth with a purpose beyond the gauge and reach of human intellect and imagination, and it is the "man of sorrows, acquainted with grief" who spends his Galilean years assuring us that this is so. His command to gather up the fragments that remained comes from his concern that everything is of value, everything is held dear to the one whose love has redemptive power to make the created order right, to make humanity better.

Only a short while ago I experienced this in the life of someone who comes here, who had been devastated and almost destroyed by a situation that overwhelmed available human wisdom. The experience was lived through, only to herald the discovery of some unexpected joy, a consolation utterly unforeseen. Fragments had indeed been divinely collected in order that nothing may be lost to that particular life. Such is the divine economy in the self-giving love that pervades the human predicament and gives purpose and insight to human existence. There is discipline in that self-giving and the discipline is the love that prompts it.

We are here to the point. You may remember how we at Saint Thomas can gratefully look back to the generous stewardship of our forebears, those who built this lovely place, born of generosity in a staggering act of profligate trust when the whole proceeds of the restoration fund after the fire had destroyed it in 1905 were given to the victims of the San Francisco earthquake in 1906, and they all began again with the result that God's promise that "the glory of this latter house shall be greater than the glory of the former house" (Haggai 2:9) was kept—and it took only a matter of days for the money to rebuild to exceed the previous total.

There is no way in which we are entitled to live on their spiritual capital, any more than we can assume their generosity to have let us off the hook. We are firmly *on* the hook. They were generous because they were poor in spirit, and were content to place their lives before God in the sacrificial giving they were moved to make. They did not hold back. We are the beneficiaries of all this, and every place you look here will remind you that this is so. I am convinced that what they learned from a generous Lord whose divine economy is disciplined by his love has to be learned afresh by every generation, and we need to learn it. Many of you give a lot. I have watched your giving grow, and have been in awe of what you have striven to do.

Others of you have been content to give less than you could and have found excellent reasons for withholding. They could be anything from disapproval of the leadership the church has been getting, either at the diocesan or the national level, or the politicizing of church programs, to things in this place which fail to satisfy, or because it is thought that we may not really need it after all. Whatever the reasons may be—and it is not my place to scold or chide—all I can and must do is to plead that you would lay seriously to heart the thing Christ says to us here in Saint Thomas, "Where a man has been given much, much will be expected of him; and the more a man has had entrusted to him the more he will be required to repay" (Luke 12:48).

Now you know what the hook is, and you realize how firmly we are on it here. You simply can't put the issue on a back burner; you can't pretend you don't understand what he's talking about, and you can't protest that it doesn't pertain to Saint Thomas.

We must tackle this business of stewardship together, you and I. We have faced a lot together over these nineteen years. My job is to let you have Christ's demands and expectations of us fairly and clearly set forth, and his "Ephphatha! Be opened!" make ears that will hear and find hearts that will welcome, and respond.

Getting Hold
of the Right End
of the Stick

As human beings we are prone to getting hold of the wrong end of the stick. We don't always get things right the first time. We can sometimes persist in holding the wrong end of the stick and not letting it go. We pass on our misinformation to others.

There was once here a very nice priest whom everybody liked to talk to and who liked to talk to everybody. He was a mine of misinformation. It made for a lot of explaining to be done without letting him down. It was hard work. And it went on for some years, so that some people went along misinformed about certain details of things for years; nothing serious, but enough to keep the rest of us busy.

Some of you will remember a parishioner here of English extraction. She was deaf and when I preached she would turn her hearing aid off. Moreover, she was among the queens of the wrong-end-of-the-stick holders. When we had to put acoustical paint on the vaulted ceiling of our nave and chancel, I had a furious letter from her demanding that we cease the project of lowering the ceiling by forty feet and putting one in that was flat. Don't ask me how she got this into her head. But it was an interesting enterprise, trying to set her right.

I have come across some wrong-end-of-the-stick sentences culled from young students' theology examination answers—though I'm sure they're not from the choir school! I give you four examples.

> 1. The Bible is full of interesting caricatures. In the first book of the Bible, Guinesses, Adam and Eve were created from an appletree. One of their children, Cain, once asked, "Am I my brother's son?"

> 2. God asked Abraham to sacrifice Isaac on Mount Montezuma. Jacob, son of Isaac, stole his brother's birth mark. Jacob was a patriarch who brought up his twelve sons to be patriarchs, but they did not take to it. One of Jacob's sons, Joseph, gave refuse to the Israelites.

> 3. Pharaoh forced the Hebrew slaves to make bread without straw. Moses led them to the Red Sea, where they made unleavened bread, which is bread without any ingredients. Afterward, Moses went up on Mount Cyanide to get the ten commandments.

> 4. David fought with the Philatelists, a race of people who lived in biblical times. Solomon, one of David's sons, had five hundred wives and five hundred porcupines.

People can indeed get hold of the wrong end of the stick. About facts. About history. About God. Supremely about God. They look into a mirror when they think about God. The God they picture has much of themselves in it. This is why God can appear vengeful, arbitrary, cruel, and judgmental. This is why he can be imagined as a sentimental old grandfather, patting our heads and telling us it doesn't matter when we try to get away with murder. Not literally, but figuratively. When we trample on his wishes and commandments and on other people he has created and whom he loves like us. When we kill the truth with deceit and lies, or strangle it so that it doesn't come out. God is not mocked. We have to be careful about facts when we deal with God so that our picture of him is not the wrong end of the stick.

The infallible way of picturing God is to look at Jesus. What Jesus is, God is. Archbishop Michael Ramsey used to say that God is Christlike and in him is no un-Christlikeness at all. What you see is what you get when you want to see God and you look at Christ. If there is anything I should like to emphasize for these fine young men who are about to leave us today after their years at the choir school, it is that. You can be sure about God when you look at Christ.

It has been a joy for us to have you among us helping to lead our worship with the magnificent music you have made. You have helped create sublime moments for us when in your singing you have brought us on occasion to the gate of heaven. Some of us, I know, are more sensitive than others in the parish family to the music you make. Some people have a tin ear. Others are grateful for the beauty you create. Include me with them. What you have done has helped to keep me going. And your choices of music this morning are magnificent.

But when you leave us for another world, another school, another set of friends, another emphasis in the educational process, we hope you can remember and will have made your own the things the choir school faculty have tried to help you apply from the picture of God you have. How you deal with other people. How you respect differences of color and race. How you have compassion for the unfortunate; the homeless, the hungry, the inadequates who depend upon your kindness and hospitality week by week in the lunches you distribute through the city on Saturday mornings. How many lunches is it now? Three hundred fifty? Is that right? The faculty have shown you what the responsibilities of privilege are, and you, like all of us, have had years of privilege in that wonderful choir school where people have tried to think of everything that would help you "grow into the measure of the stature of the fulness of Christ," as Saint Paul says.

I can't think of instructors for people your age who could have done the job better than our choir school faculty. I was talking to a beautiful girl this past week who is my goddaughter, and she is named for her great granny, Cricket. She was telling me how formative *her* school was, and how it has enriched her life and how gratefully she views it in the totality of her present life. It will be a good thing to see you in the years ahead in the lives you embrace, helped by what you have experienced here to have the right end of the stick in your understanding of God and his people in your life. It may be that you join schools and make friends with people who haven't had as much exposure to the church as you have had, who don't know as much as you about music or singing or math, or God.

It may be that you, just by being yourself, can help them. They may be like the people we read about in the gospels who say to Christ's disciples, "Sir, we want to see Jesus!" And they may catch a glimpse of him in you. They may catch a glimpse of his joy in you. It is part of his plan that you discover it in your life. You will discover it when you play hard and play fair, physically and mentally pitting your strength in a challenge presented to you. You will discern it in winning; and strange to say, you *can* discern it in losing. You will discover it as you exploit your creativity, making things, solving things. You *can* discover it in sickness and in failure. I have seen that. You will, I hope, soon discover it when you fall in love and are loved in return. You *can* discover it in solitude and silence. It is there for you to discover, and people will see it and hope to have something like that in their lives. If you "look to Jesus," as Paul says, you will find him. Or better still, and more accurately, he will find you. He is waiting to do just that.

When I was in Italy some weeks ago, I saw an intriguing notice in queer English in the hotel telephone instruction book. It said, "How to get the eternal line." I'm still not quite sure what the Italian expression is, but I think I know what the notice meant to convey. The eternal line means the *external* line, I guess. For us, the eternal line is Christ. He is our line to God, eternally open, eternally available, eternally accurate, and eternally true. Use him, and you will never get the wrong end of the stick about God and the world. Use him, and you will never be told you have the wrong number!

Finding Yourself
on Another Path

The wife of a friend of mine announced last Tuesday that she proposed to become a Roman Catholic on Friday. This she did, in the Cardinal Archbishop of Westminster's house during the Mass in his chapel, and her family were with her to witness this. She has long been a devout Anglican, born into a staunch Anglican family, and her spiritual journey began years ago after a tragedy in her life. She has left the church of her birth and family without losing her affection for it, but propelled by a deep movement of the spirit within her soul to find a home in another place.

This is something that happens to people that affects others. This parish family has said goodbye to souls whose journeys have taken them from us to join another church. I can think of at least four people in my time here who have felt the movement of the spirit within their soul and have been obedient to its promptings and have done the very same thing as my friend's wife did.

The lessons today tell of the urgings of the spirit. Samuel as a small boy becomes vividly aware—as if he hears a human voice calling his name—that he must begin a spiritual journey. God met him in the night, and called him by his name: "Samuel! Samuel!"

And then John tells us of Philip's excitement at being discovered. Christ finds Philip. Philip doesn't stumble into Christ. Christ meets Philip and puts to him a personal challenge to follow him. Christ confronts Philip with an offer of friendship and companionship as a disciple. Philip's soul is stirred to accept the offer, and he receives the challenge to personal commitment to Jesus. The acceptance affects somebody else: Nathaniel, Philip's friend, to whom Philip goes with the news of the confrontation and his own personal discovery that he has "met the man spoken of by Moses in the Law, and by the prophets: it is Jesus son of Joseph, from Nazareth" (John 1:45).

Philip's soul-journey takes an unexpected direction and he repudiates his friend's rude comment on Nazareth by persuading him to "come and see." The meeting and the subsequent call to follow the carpenter's son from Nazareth, the one of whom Moses and the prophets spoke, intervene in lives going one way, but now pursuing another.

There are certain things you have to do. One of these things is to follow your conscience. If you become certain in your heart that you should choose a path different from the one you happen to be on, even though your conscience is as fallible and flawed as the rest of your personhood is—as fallible and flawed as every other human being's—then you have to do what you have to do. It may be a mistake. It may be the wrong turning in the road to take. But not to pursue what in the deepest depth of your heart you know you should pursue can land you in a serious moral dilemma in which you are likely to be culpable.

Many of you sitting here and listening to this have in your lifetime made a decision to become an Episcopalian. You have been brought up to tread another denominational path. You may have been brought up not even to bother to tread *any* denominational path. Some of you might have started out as not merely uncaring about the spiritual life within you but actively hostile to the very concept of a spiritual life.

Some of you may have incurred the disapproval and hostility of your family and your spouse when you were convinced to make this move. Some of you may have had motives imputed to you for making it which do you no credit at all. Whatever the reasons and circumstances and events that led you to think in terms which brought you to this decision, there came a day and an hour when the die was cast, and determination took over and you set your face despite the consequences, and you did it. And when you did it, the new scene and your place in it was not necessarily easy or pleasant or what you expected. But having crossed the Rubicon, having burned your boats behind you, you persevered. And here you are.

But you brought your history with you. You carried the marks of your pilgrimage, its strains and its scars. You carried the wounds of the decision to make the move. You carried all the luggage of a life so far lived, with you. Some of it will be useful. It will provide you with insights that cradle Episcopalians may never have stopped to think might be there.

These insights will be the gifts you bring to the faith, something which will enrich my faith, perhaps, as your pastor and parish priest and servant and teacher, as well as the faith of the people you meet up with here in Saint Thomas, your worshiping companions. You have to assess these insights critically, however. Will this insight light up or diminish the faith of myself and my companions on the journey together? So your humility and wisdom will be tested.

It is simply no good being a Baptist with an Anglican overcoat on. Every denomination contains within itself the seeds of its own ruination—a chilling reminder to take seriously. For some denomination it can be complacency; for another it can be judgmentalism; for another it can be materialism under the camouflage of blessings received for good behavior; for another it can involve leaving your brains at home while others deemed as infallible do your thinking for you. There are many disappointing aspects in each particular denomination. And no denomination is perfect.

Certainly I would consider suspect a denomination which lays proprietary claim to all truth. Saint Paul tells us to "prove all things." So your insights have to be tested by you as valid contributions to the faith you have embraced. It does us good to remember that the process of discovery never ends on this side of life's river. I find that my Anglicanism is constantly being refined and realigned to some extent by what I discover in you and the way you live your faith.

Along with testing what you have brought along with you, there is the business of *forgetting*. Forgetting is part of our pilgrimage. Who says so? Saint Paul says so.

Forgetting what is behind me, and reaching out for that which lies ahead, I press towards the goal to win the prize which is God's call to the life above, in Christ Jesus. (Philippians 3:13-14)

God's call involves a forgetting on our part. What is there
to forget as we make the decision to move forward out of
obedience to the conscience which brings us from one
path to another?

It may well be that we ought to forget our certitudes,
our brass-bound confidence that we have had the right
answers to things about God and about people and our
judgments of them and their motives; our certainties that
God's authority and truth are firmly behind our judgments of situations and people. It may be that we should
forget to boast about how far we have grown spiritually,
implying that others haven't kept pace with our growth. It
may be that we should forget the injuries we have sustained from those who consider themselves spiritually or
socially or intellectually superior to us, and press on, with
forgiveness rather than rancor in our sights, and a desire
to justify ourselves, to prove ourselves acceptable.

It may well be that part of the process of forgetting
what is behind is learning to forgive ourselves for tread-
ing another path than the one we are now on, and to accept the fact that *we are accepted of God,* all forgiven by
that boundless ocean of love which flows from the sacred
heart of Christ, as we look to Jesus. For in doing what in
conscience we have to do, if we look to Christ as we do it,
his companionship will sustain us and his hand will
steady us, his body will nourish us and his voice will call
us to the place he has gone ahead to prepare for us.

CHRIST
THE KING

Much is made here of the feast of Christ the King, which is traditionally kept on the last Sunday before Advent. The great carved stone figure of our Lord crowned in majesty as King and High Priest dominates the reredos at Saint Thomas, and there is an atmosphere of anticipation and joy as kingly music floods the liturgy for this final celebration of the Christian year.

Naught For Your Comfort

A s you heard read the Scriptures set for today, the last Sunday before Advent begins, you may have felt an unwelcome draught. They talk of separation and sundering. There is enough talk of it to dismay you. The love God has for us isn't a sticky sentimental glue adhering us in one uncomfortable mass, fastening us to him at the cost of his integrity. The love God has for us makes it perfectly clear that separation is part of it all because his truth *is* his love, and his truth cannot countenance anything less than truth in us. Nothing is hidden from him.

I call this day "Separation Sunday." Listen to what Ezekiel the prophet says in the last verse of the Old Testament lesson:

> And as for you, O my flock, thus saith the Lord God; Behold, I judge between cattle and cattle, between the rams and he-goats. (Ezekiel 34:17)

Between cattle and cattle. Some go this way. Others are sent that way. In the word-picture of a herdsman and a shepherd, God intends to deal with his people *and make choices.* There is selection. There is separation. Rams, one way; he-goats, another.

This is something we have to come to terms with. And
Christ hammers this theme home—and I use that expression advisedly—in the gospel when he says:

> "When the Son of Man comes in his glory and all the an-
> gles with him, he will sit in state on his throne, with all
> the nations gathered before him. He will separate men
> into two groups, as a shepherd separates the sheep from
> the goats, and he will place the sheep on his right hand
> and the goats on his left." (Matthew 25:31-33)

We have to face the likelihood, not just the notion, of
exclusion and loss, separation and sundering, in Christ's
dealings with us. I am not being an alarmist. I am not
preaching fire and brimstone. I am telling you what Scripture says. I am telling you what Christ says. The coming
of Christ in judgment will be no pretty sight. Answerabil-
ity, accountability, explanation are the terms of it for us.

Some will be near his companionship, others will feel
the lack. His term for it is *on his right,* and *on his left.* And
the grounds of his judgment are what we do with the opportunities given to us to love at the deepest level within
ourselves. It is a gut responsibility and our instinct is usually for self-protection, so that the words "charity begins
at home" spring to the lips. But charity doesn't begin at
home.

Christ is the first and last to insist that charity doesn't
begin at home. It begins and ends in him; in his heart of
love, in which all Creation has a place, a treasured place.
Always when we mouth the phrase "enlightened self-interest" we have to watch out of the corner of our eyes for
where Christ is pointing, to his *right* or to his *left,* whether
the phrase is prudent politically or not.

Talking about enlightened self-interest—what do you happen to think of a nuisance that can frighten you, like the hordes of homeless begging in the Grand Central or Penn stations or the Port Authority, or in the subway trains you have to take? Don't be sentimental and suggest that because they have nothing they aren't capable of sin. There are deeper questions to consider. They are a threat to our ease, a nasty reminder thrust under our noses. Banish them? Where do you banish them to? Where are they to go? What are we to do with people who are reduced to subhumanity, either through drugs or through no fault of their own? You can't lock them up. You can't banish them elsewhere. They constitute for us a problem of frightening proportions, in all sorts of ways. No easy answer of enlightened self-interest. They are the least of God's little ones. But then....

> "Then he will say to those on his left hand, 'The curse is upon you; go from my sight to the eternal fire that is ready for the devil and his angels. For when I was hungry you gave me nothing to eat, when thirsty nothing to drink; when I was a stranger you gave me no home, when naked you did not clothe me; when I was ill and in prison you did not come to my help.'
>
> "And they too will reply, 'Lord, when was it that we saw you hungry or thirsty or a stranger or naked or ill or in prison, and did nothing for you?'
>
> "And he will answer, 'I tell you this: anything you did not do for one of these, however humble, you did not do for me.'" (Matthew 25:41-45)

And that is not all. Christ ends with something that is not a threat but a promise:

"And they will go away to eternal punishment, but the righteous will enter eternal life." (Matthew 25:46)

We might wish he had not said this, but we can't pretend he hasn't. We have to face a possibility of Christ disassociating himself from attitudes and enterprises of our own manufacture, turning his back on policies we maintain, and refusing to countenance our rationalizing selfishness, however sophisticated it may be in its disguise. It is easier to point to the appalling philosophy of Marxism, or to the cruel policies of apartheid, or to the callous side of capitalism, or whatever it is which meets with our own disapproval. We can attempt to write a gospel which oversimplifies issues we can't cope with, or wish to see extinct. But this is not Christ's way. The buck stops here. We cannot find shelter behind stern words of judgment of somebody else. What is Christ saying to the whole family, his church?

He may be saying something like this: the church is under judgment even though it is his body; the church militant, composed as it is of living souls, can no more disregard this terrible warning than individuals can hope to disregard it. If, for whatever reason of self-interest the church fails to reach out with love and with compassion to those outside her bounds—the doubting, the alienated, the hurt, even those with self-inflicted hurts, people with lifestyles we neither like or think the church should countenance—then she is in danger of failing.to notice Christ shining through the eyes of those unsuitable souls.

Wherever goodness of the very least sort is, Christ is. In mixed-up, mistaken, errant, ignorant, bigoted, backward souls—wherever a spark of goodness is, it is the Spirit of Christ who makes that spirit glow. When she is tempted to categorize and pigeonhole and brand with a mark, she runs the risk of exclusion from Christ's companionship. Her job is to offer the stern challenge of reconciliation to irreconcilables, bringing in the unwilling with the offer of love and the recalcitrant with the promise of God's for-giveness, and proclaiming to all souls everywhere Christ's sovereignty and kingship, which conveys to an incredu-lous world of individuals the means of grace and the hope of glory.

Cowley Publications is a ministry of the Society of St. John the Evangelist, a religious community for men in the Episcopal Church. Emerging from the Society's tradition of prayer, theological reflection, and diversity of mission, the press is centered in the rich heritage of the Anglican Communion.

Cowley Publications seeks to provide books, audio cassettes, and other resources for the ongoing theological exploration and spiritual development of the Episcopal Church and others in the body of Christ. To this end, it is dedicated to developing a new generation of theological writers, encouraging them to produce timely, creative, and stimulating publications of excellence, and making these publications available widely, reaching both clergy and lay persons.